Trend

a pattern of life

Trend

a pattern of life

observed and written by
Sue Rinaldi

HODDER & STOUGHTON
LONDON SYDNEY AUCKLAND

First published in Great Britain 1999

The right of Sue Rinaldi to be identified as the Author
of the Work has been asserted by her in accordance with the
Copyright, Designs and Patents Act 1988

.

10 9 8 7 6 5 4 3 2 1

British Library Cataloguing in Publication Data
A record for this book is available from
the British Library

ISBN 0 340 72215 0

Printed and bound in Great Britain by
Clays

Hodder and Stoughton Ltd
A Division of Hodder Headline PLC
338 Euston Road
London NW1 3BH

trendthe elements

the observatory

going green, eco-warriors, nature's bounty, the chemical generation, designer medicine, generation ecstasy, food for thought, bodytalk, transformation, size matters, fashion, it's good to talk, paradise on earth, love@aol, addicted to love, game on, public displays of confession, a religious image, icons and idols, fake society, promise land

lookout

Trends are

mysterious, predictable, unaccountable,
interchangeable, cultural, temporal,
unexplainable, explainable,
analysed, believable, tempting, influential,
reflective, prophetic, nostalgic, twisting, radical,
safe, commercial, money making, fascinating,
history making, life changing, powerful, fun,
disempowering, foreseeable

A Pattern of Life

we can create trend or be created by trend
effect trend or be affected by trend
ignore trend or be ignored

trendthe credits

Trend is the result, so far, of my fascination with life, culture and people. As well as my own comments and critiques, it also reflects the thoughts and theories of other writers, history makers and iconoclasts who, by their very desire to war against indifference, have made their mark upon my life and more importantly upon society. *Trend* also looks at the lighter side of life – yes I have been convinced that there is one! – and observes those little eccentricities which provoke us to laugh at ourselves. A quality I firmly believe to be more invaluable in this age than ever before.

Trend is not an in-depth research book. There are plenty of those around written by clever and informed people. It is more an overview of current events and beliefs, a word-bite adventure of a culture in crisis, a micro-media programme investigating issues which affect you and me.

Whilst every effort has been made to correctly acknowledge my sources, and to seek the necessary copyright permissions, I have in a few cases been unable to trace the original reference. The publisher will be happy to print the correct acknowledgement in future editions of the book.

Thanks to the many people who have influenced, challenged and informed my thinking over the years. People like Linda Harding, Elaine Storkey, Patrick Dixon, Phil Wall, Gerald Coates and Christine Noble. My good friend and musician Caroline

Bonnett, who along with other musicians, Kevin Prosch and Martin Smith, has inspired and provoked and above all, given me glimpses of another world.

This book is far more than the sum total of my thoughts – I am so grateful to other writers and thinkers who have dared to commit to paper their own thoughts, hopes and dreams. People like Martin Scott, John Drane, Simone de Beauvoir and countless others who have left their mark upon my imagination. Special mention also to those who write for the *New Internationalist* magazine – their hunger for justice is infectious!

Credit is also due to Robyn Blood who spent many hours scrutinising the manuscript for grammatical errors and readability, and to Julie Rose who painstakingly catalogued hundreds of articles. There's more to come!

But *Trend* is about life – so maximum gratitude goes to the giver of life.

The Making of Trend

a fashion statement

> fashions, after all, are induced epidemics
> – george bernard shaw [1]

Our world overflows with colour and variety, diversity and inventiveness. Yet so often we feel under pressure to conform – to act the same, look the same and sound the same. There's often a dominant culture which anaesthetises our sense of innovation. So rather than celebrate diversity, we hide it away and become a slave to fashion or prevailing directions.

There seems to be a tension within every human being – the yearning to be individual, yet the need to belong. This inherent need to belong or even conform can create patterns of behaviour which identify themselves en masse as obvious directions or trends.

deep needs

> we are all born originals but die copies
> – gerald coates, author

There seems to be a heartfelt need within each individual for community, a place to belong. This is a positive element of the human race – our dependence and interdependence upon one another – even though at times we do not like to admit it! Maybe this is what drives an individual to adopt a certain hairstyle, clothing, bodyart, language or behaviour in order to fit in and be recognised as belonging to an identifiable group? How often do we look at past photographs of ourselves and cringe with embarrassment at making such a bad fashion statement? However, on the negative side, there are times when personal discretion or dignity is compromised and ignored in order to be part of the action. How often do we regret the things we have said and done because of the pressure to be accepted as one of the crowd?

There are behavioural trends that people follow and each decade has a story to tell.

from genesis to revolution

The 1950s gave rise to a people group recognisable by the quasi-Edwardian clothes they wore and the music they listened to. These Teddy Boys were trendsetters and important in that they sprang up during the genesis of a collective tribe now classified as 'teenager'. Unlike any time before it, teenagers now became a recognised group within society. They had more money for people of their age than at any other time in history and the manufacturers jumped onto this, creating and influencing demand. As Steve Sutherland quotes in his article for *New Musical Express*, 'You could argue that the very notion of teenage rebellion was created in the late 50's by marketing men eager to extract cash from a gullible and, for the first time, financially independent young market … creating tribes to sell records and clothing'. [2]

Soon after, the teen scene became more complex. The Swinging

12

Sixties, notorious for being a time of experimentation with people courageously speaking out for freedom and liberation, soon divided and subdivided into many more history changing tribes including mods, rockers and hippies. Each with different images, different ideologies and different musical tastes, every subculture was set apart from the other. There was intense rivalry between these distinctive groups and adults were shocked to see the varying displays of teenage rebellion. However, trends in music, clothing, language, behaviour and morality were becoming noticed and firmly established.

> youth culture of that era was all pervasive. it overthrew old taboos, filled young breasts with optimism and made teenagers believe that the world was in their hands. a thrilling time, and the values absorbed by the people who grew up in it seem, in many cases, never quite to have been sloughed off
> – **clive aslet** [3]

The seventies introduced more subcultures to the stage, with skinheads and punks being the principal actors. But reality bites and as unemployment loomed and social issues came to the fore, it became more urgent to analyse and understand the whole subject of trends. As well as simply talking musical or clothing differences, the stakes of disillusionment and progression increased. Racism, hooliganism, feminism, sexual behaviour – patterns of behaviour became a vital and fascinating study.

> a person becomes defined by what he or she is against – **nme** [2]

The eighties were even more fragmented. Rockers were still

around, mods came back into fashion, punks were occasionally spotted, rastas, goths, new romantics and a myriad of others jumped on board. There was a greater emphasis upon expressing individuality and this indulgence gave permission for the 'anything goes' philosophy to become the normal and respected framework upon which to live life. Existentialism – the belief that truth depends on your own personal experience – thrived in an environment which delighted in being different. Also, many of those who grew up in the Swinging Sixties were now in places of influence and their laissez-faire philosophy to morality was remarkably evident.

> **the picture's getting smaller with each trend
> – *nme*** [2]

The nineties exploded in everyone's face, as the human race realised it was in crisis, reaping the mistakes of the experimentation of the last decades. Sexual crisis, environmental crisis, social crisis, ethical crisis, spiritual crisis, physical crisis – these became the trends that would jitterbug across people groups and affect you whatever the colour of your hair or the make of your shoes.

The outworkings of this new found legalisation of non-conformity are that the subcultures have become less distinct, and sharing aspects of each other's identity is in vogue. Now we are experiencing the hybrid fever, where groups mix and match style and sound, making it permissible to dress surf-style, listen to Celine Dion and campaign for animal rights all at the same time. Although this appears acceptable to many, it does have its critics. 'A rather dull consensus of cool has begun to form about music, culture, fashion and lifestyle', says *NME*, 'and a lot of that is a result and a reflection of the decline of tribalism, as manifested in the amorphous but nevertheless fiercely identifiable subcultures which have traditionally dominated British pop culture. We're going to need a new movement of people, styles and ideas to shake things up.' [2]

Sexual crisis, environmental crisis, social crisis, ethical crisis, spiritual crisis, physical crisis – these became the trends that would jitterbug across people groups and affect you whatever the colour of your hair or the make of your shoes.

the times they are a changin'

trends have a life cycle. they are sown or fertilised, they gestate, they grow, mature, age and eventually die. some trends are reincarnated a decade or more later, often in slightly different form – *next* by ira matathia and marian salzman [4]

This rough guide to the last four decades reveals them to be unique times, highly original and innovatory, with new birth at every twist and turn. To hope again for such times could be cultural suicide or just wishful thinking. What is more fascinating is that even in this tribal cross-pollination the trends keep coming. But instead of trends only formulating within one identifiable people group, which incidentally still occurs, they are also spread broadly across the people groups. For example, a call for purer sexual behaviour will be heard from people who cross many socio-economic groups but have a longing and conviction to face the consequences of promiscuity and the effect of broken relationships. Ethical and spiritual trends are increasingly cross-tribal.

Ethical and spiritual trends are increasingly cross-tribal.

15

tribes of a different kind

> youth is something anyone of any age can buy into by appropriating the right brand names, clubs or magazines. nowadays being in a tribe called youth doesn't mean bonding around a counter-cultural experience ... it merely means sharing a set of consumer experiences
> – nilgin yusuf, teenage kicks, *scene* magazine, jan/feb 1999

Trends are still observed within distinctive sociological tribes or groups, and advertisers attempt to target these tribes in order to sell products and influence spending and consumer choice. 'Trendtracking is critical to the marketing process. Accurately spotting and forecasting trends is of fundamental importance in determining whether an ad is a genuine asset to a brand or simply a negligible wave over which channel surfers pass,' [4] write Matathia and Salzman in their book *Next*. Companies are very careful about the type of music they choose for their advertisement – the slogan, the image, the logo – in order to capitalise on a prevailing trend or even instigate a new one. Never underestimate the power of an advert.

Great slogans like 'don't imitate, innovate', 'image is nothing, thirst is everything', 'one day tenderness will change the world' become synonymous with the product and also the supposed lifestyle of its target audience. Successful products can simply flash the brand icon and instinctively consumers know what is being advertised. A great deal of research is conducted in order to understand what trends and cultural shifts are taking place.

For example, the makers of Thickhead, the alco-pop drink, researched and defined six types of youth within youth culture in order to target their product at the right person. It is interesting to note that these 'types' are far less identifiable by clothing style and music and more identifiable by ethical and spiritual belief. The tribes have become bigger and wider and at times even turn into generations – chemical, wired, jilted or otherwise. Tribes within tribes, with individuals belonging to two or three or more. Thickhead discovered the:

Cyber Gen:	techno literate and techno hungry, the wired generation
Cerebral:	with pastimes such as reading and Internet surfing
Eco-Pagan:	encompassing holistic science, cult religions, alternative medicine, free festivals and eco-anarchy
A-Gender:	with the blurring of gender distinctions reflected in a growing androgyny in fashion
Glam Bang:	with retro seventies style and a post-modern sense of irony
Street Sport:	where sports, entertainment and street fashion collide

Each identified group obviously had certain recognisable qualities and Thickhead no doubt picked up on the general directions and tendencies of each group.

Never underestimate the power of an advert.

retrospect

what goes around comes around, it's history repeating itself
– shirley bassey and the propellerheads

Trends are part of life. They come and go … and return again. Revamped, repackaged and selling under another name! There is a fascination with all things retro and this can be seen with clothing, music, furniture and even children's names. It is interesting to observe that new styles of clothing are often based upon designs of the past. For example, a modern taste for flared trousers is looked upon incredulously by those who wore them the first time around. Is the future in the past? Have we all simply run out of ideas? Why now more than any other time in history are people anxious to go back to their roots? And why is there so much talk about revival? A fifties revival in furniture, a sixties revival in clothing and a seventies revival in music?

> **Trends are part of life. They come and go … and return again. Revamped, repackaged and selling under another name!**

revival

The r-word is being used in many different contexts. There has obviously been the rebirth of seventies music, and the circular turn of events that has saved vinyl albums from extinction, allowing the discs to spin again and be promoted as a 'happening format'. And what about the sixties-style wardrobe that was once only kept to supply you and your friends with a handy outfit for fancy dress parties but now advantageously rated to be highly fashionable! And how ironic it is that whilst retro is 'in', we can now design our house interior to look just like something our parents once lived in without fear of being mocked, misunderstood or embarrassed.

On the other hand this revival word is also being used to describe the re-awakening of religious fervour that is happening on a global scale. Even the mainstream press and television companies are documenting the signs of the nineties faith revival, transmitting life-changing stories and spiritual energy into the living room, causing people to sit up and take notice.

going back to my roots

> could we maybe get things right by leaping backwards into our own history, and seeking to rediscover afresh the kind of worldview that motivated our long-forgotten ancestors? this possibly accounts for the renewed interest in ancient celtic spirituality, goddess worship and the increasing popularity of neo-paganism in its many forms, all of which are perhaps the fastest growing types of popular spirituality in northern europe today – **john drane** [5]

It appears satisfying to relive elements of the past within a different framework – but there seems more to this retrospection than that. Maybe the future is so unknown that people wish for familiar anchor points. Maybe the heartfelt longing for roots is because people are hungry for a sense of belonging.

In the December 1998 edition of *Frank* magazine, Margit J. Mayer commented, 'Christ is making a comeback. At the dawn of a new millennium there is a growing feeling of being both overwhelmed and spiritually undernourished by today's secular trinity of Ambition, Information and Style. It's only logical that Christianity will make a comeback.' [6] Harriet Quick also remarks in the same edition of *Frank*, 'religion, if not at the forefront of fashionable minds in the late 20th century, is at least lurking around.' [7]

Publishing the King James Version of the Bible as separate books has been an immense hit. Claire Paterson, editor of the series, explains, 'our aim was to make what is probably the most important book in English literature more accessible and easier to read.' [8]

> everyone is on the hunt for god ... from the four
> corners of the earth, people are coming to their
> senses, are running back to yahweh
> – Psalm 22, the bible, *message* version

Maybe the future is so unknown that people wish for familiar anchor points.

restless pilgrims

> the celts ... saw themselves as part of their
> community – family, clan, nation. there was an
> intrinsic spirituality and a ready belief in 'the
> supernatural'. celtic christians were mystical and
> instinctively creative. they loved nature for its own
> sake, and saw god's fingerprints there
> – roger ellis and chris seaton, *new celts* [9]

There has been a growing interest in Celtic spirituality, which appears to reflect the search for personal roots of belonging. Academic interest, spiritual pilgrimages to sacred sites, and music and dance similar to *Riverdance* has brought the flavour and belief of Celtic spirituality into the mainstream. Why has the ancient become modern?

Chris Seaton and Roger Ellis explain in their book *New Celts*,

> a millennial mood often causes people to look to their roots.
> The year 1997 represented a remarkable anniversary, and the
> nation was reminded of its Christian ancestors by a set of

commemorative postage stamps. Fourteen centuries ago, in 597, one of the greatest of the Celtic saints, Columba, died on Iona. In the same year Pope Gregory's special envoy, Augustine of Canterbury, landed on the Kent coast with a mission to convert the heathen Anglo-Saxons. Also, the phenomenon known as post-modernity has taken a thorough grip on our culture in the Nineties. Post-modernity challenges every certainty and every statement of accepted wisdom. The concepts of 'borrowing' and 're-inventing' have become more important than a quest for originality. [10]

Why has the ancient become modern?

post-modern

> we are the first post-modern generation ...
> described as having no sense of heritage or history
> and little hope for a better future
> – mike pilavachi [11]

There is a constant pursuit for appropriate words and phrases to describe the varying conditions within society adequately. This last decade, I'm sure, has collected more 'buzz words' than at any other time in history. Modern, post-modern, hypermodern: can we detect a way through this 'thoroughly modern millennium' maze?

Modernism has its roots in the eighteenth-century Enlightenment. With its emphasis on human reason and rational thinking, the predominant view was that science and technology were the instruments of progress and that mixed together with human ingenuity, a brave new world would be constructed. Modernism peaked in the middle of this century and, by 1960, many were questioning the values of society and saw that the great positives were matched by some frightening negatives. The climate is now 'post-modern'.

> these post-modern years are symptomatic of a total lack of originality. our scanty resources of invention are all parasitically confined to reproduction. everything apparently 'new' whether it be CDs, cyberspace, or virtual reality, is feeding on the originality of the past, on a data bank not simply of information but of already experienced reality
> – *postmodernism for beginners* [12]

Post-modernism does not necessarily introduce a single fresh idea, but is descriptive of the society we live in. Fast images, interactive videos, information technology, irrational beliefs, relativism, a lack of absolutes, installation art, androgyny, reality in the shape of a company logo, iconic images – these are all signs and symbols of a continuous contemporary culture.

Hypermodernism is yet another play on words. According to the book *Postmodernism for Beginners*, hypermodernism is 'a technological hyper-intensification of modernism. Technology and economics merge and are disguised by alternative labels – post industrial, electronic, services, information, computer economy – each of which contributes to hyper-real processing and simulation.' [13]

Whether all this is just psycho-babble responding to a changing culture or the result of successful marketing straplines, there is one thing of which you can be sure: new, descriptive phrases are absolutely certain to occur in copious amounts in the foreseeable future. Our challenge is to keep in step with the pace of this change and try to understand where the human being fits in this techno-logical, hyper-logical, cyber-logical age!

Modern, post-modern, hypermodern: can we detect a way through this 'thoroughly modern millennium' maze?

generation next

> my generation is the warm-up act for the 21st century, not the curtain call for the 20th. we defy the ironic/post-ironic, post-modern/post-post-modern tags that get stuck on us because we don't consider ourselves 'post' anything. we're 'pre' everything exciting that will happen in the next few years — **polly wiseman, talking 'bout my generation,** *scene* **magazine, jan/feb 1999**

Generation X has been the in-phrase for a while now. Over the last few years, social observers have analysed the inherent behavioural patterns of X-ers whilst advertising companies have had an incredibly lucrative time gearing the right product and money-catching slogan to this visible generation.

In 1991, Douglas Coupland wrote *Generation X – Tales for an Accelerated Culture*. A book about Andy, Dag and Clare, 'twenty-somethings, brought up with divorce, Watergate and Three Mile Island, and scarred by the 80's fallout of yuppies, recession, crack and Ronald Reagan, they represent the new generation – Generation X.' [14] This book was a landmark and the media pounced on one of the widest-used buzz phrases of the last decade.

Generation X became a descriptive title for the culture and values of those born in the sixties and seventies. The world was introduced to some excellent observations:

option paralysis –   the tendency when given unlimited choices, to make none

me-ism –	a search by the individual for a personally tailored religion
black holes –	a sub group known to possess an almost entirely black wardrobe
the cult of aloneness –	the need for autonomy at all costs even at the expense of long-term relationships
decade blending –	the indiscriminate combination of two or more items of clothing from various decades to create a personal mood

The X culture is full of contradictions and cynicism, where objective truth becomes an impossible commodity. With no sense of community, technology has replaced human relationships and bombarded by images of violence and injustice, emotions are anaesthetised. But the inevitable has happened – an even newer generation has emerged.

The X culture is full of contradictions and cynicism, where objective truth becomes an impossible commodity.

generation y

Generation Y has officially been recognised and the American Trends' analysts have already labelled this generation born since the early 1980s as upbeat and confident. Australian reporter Polly Wilson explains, 'they are optimists who have grown up comfortable with technology, expert button pushers, many have their own mobile phones and are more at home on the Internet than their parents.' [15]

However, it's the younger members of this generation that are the most fascinating. It seems that these are the ones who have the real purchasing power, even though they are too young to earn money. These 'Millennials' know what they want and in particular what brand they want and will not settle for anything less. Manufacturers are targeting this age group and getting incredible results as parents supply the demands of these trend conscious youngsters. These trends are changing faster than ever and in an instant Barbie gets replaced by a Spice Girl and even Tinky Winky gets ousted for a 128-bit Crash Bandicoot computer game.

'You are what you wear' has been a cultural proverb for many years, but for *Generation Y* it is even more consuming. 'You are what you buy' takes that prevailing 'truth' many steps forward and creates utopia for the product manufacturers as they watch the child market multiply, as twelves and unders make a definite shift into the power seat, particularly in the lucrative technology market.

It is alarming to see the products being formulated for the *Generation Y* toddlers. The assumption is that they now accompany their parents on more activities previously categorised as adult. So we can order the 'babychino' in coffee shops – frothy milk with chocolate powder on top and no coffee – and even choose a suitable perfume from many of the top French fragrance houses who are introducing children's perfume ranges.

Is it too much to hope that *Generation Y* will have learnt something from the X-ers? Will this new generation actually emerge more concerned with ethics than labels, and not allow themselves to be dictated to by the fashion houses and advertisers? If the Ys succumb, will we then have to wait for 'Generation Z' to be the deliberately different generation?

Will this new generation actually emerge more concerned with ethics than labels … ?

millennials

Others are classifying these eighties conceptions as the 'Millennial Generation'. A MORI and Adam Smith Institute survey published in November 1998 comments, 'British 16 to 21 year-olds are more classless, meritocratic and self-reliant than any other age group. The picture painted is of a generation which differs in many respects from its predecessors. They do not expect too much from the political process and accord little or no respect to its practitioners.' The report concludes, 'The Millennial Generation seem to be self-confident and self-dependent. They aim high and do not think themselves limited by background.' [16]

Advertisers often play the role of popular prophet, speaking with catchphrases and symbols into the core of culture. St Nike's encouragement to the masses to 'Just Do It' has recently been changed to 'I Can'. Perhaps this shift of emphasis succinctly summarises the change in temperature between the X and the Y Generation.

2000 and beyond

> they told us we would have holidays on the moon, use robots in the kitchen, and travel to work by rocket packs. instead we got 'centerparcs', microwave ovens and rollerblades
> – rupert howe, *the face* [17]

The overwhelming emphasis placed upon the new century has meant that 1999 is quickly fading into insignificance amid the millennium talk and clock-watching nervousness. The close of a century is a unique time for reflection, contemplation and evaluation, with an obvious fascination for predicting what life will be like in the new millennium.

Despite reasonable fears about the 'Y2K millennium bug' and what exactly this brave new world we have created will deliver, the global celebrations planned speak of confidence, high energy and optimism, and all this millennium fever will hopefully deal a death blow to the last-days-flavour of cynical disillusionment of the age that has just departed.

One thing is sure: change is here to stay. Trends reveal movement and progression, they also exhibit a regressive tendency to be repeated time and again, in newly enhanced formats. Whatever trends we observe and adopt, I hope that we learn from the lessons of the past. To reconstruct twenty-first-century versions of injustice, hatred and exploitation is unforgivable, but to birth or rebirth quirks of fashion or patterns of life is ... predictable.

The close of a century is a unique time for reflection, contemplation and evaluation ...

✝ Spiritzone

time for change [1]

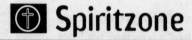

it's a new dawn for britain – **tony blair**

Positive words to herald a new phase for this country or simply wishful thinking from an election winner? Tony Blair was seen by many to be the political saviour of the masses and whether or not you agree with his party politics, the sentiment behind his post-victory phrase accurately described the heartbeat of a nation.

The need for change is being expressed by all kinds of people from all walks of life. With urgency and persistency we are hearing the same message from different voices. Almost every day we hear the cries from many activist groups shouting loud and clear for environmental change, social change, educational change, justice … the issues may be different but the message is the same – enough is enough!

A leading tabloid paper featured evidence from a best-selling author who has apparently discovered a hidden code in the Bible. He claims to have unlocked this code and not only does it predict every major event in history but more importantly it may reveal the future of humankind. As disillusionment with the present age increases, interest in the future age becomes stronger.

There is a strong inclination to predict the future, and fathom the unfathomable. Television programmes like *Crystal Balls* reflect this interest, as they look back on the accuracy of past predictions and prophets, and project into the future. The media in general is adding fuel to the already considerable fire of fascination, as we stand on the edge of a new century.

At an international Christian event in Norwich in 1997, the cry from the 5,000 people attending was remarkably similar. From the youngest to the oldest, there was the realisation that this once 'great' Britain could be about to sink under the weight of hopelessness and despair, where violence, abuse, pain and loneliness have contributed to the desire for change. Without change, the future looks bleak. Many are therefore aligning themselves to a new rhythm of faith and have adopted the title of 'revival generation' to explain their vision of hope. Throwing off the self-indulgent and destructive values of their counterparts, like old unwanted clothes, they are voluntarily choosing a new wardrobe. Desperate to see a revival of dignity, equality, purity and purpose, this new generation, which encompasses every age group, is unashamedly living out their lives as followers of a more established world leader – Jesus Christ.

People everywhere are longing to breathe a different air and see society cleansed from the pollution of hedonism. Amidst all the variables of life, there is one thing becoming constant; the persistent sound of voices calling for a restoration of morality, family values and respect for one another. This is the only way a nation in darkness will see a new dawn.

In order to appreciate the spiritual uprising of the last two decades more fully, one must wander down history a little to see some of the influences upon modern society.

As disillusionment with the present age increases, interest in the future age becomes stronger.

the journey of belief

> a new age of spirituality is upon us. it is now very acceptable to turn to inner resources or outside powers for enrichment and survival – **anon**

During the eighteenth century the Church was at the centre of life and it set the standards for 'normal' lifestyle and ethical behaviour, thus creating a Christianised society. This resulted in fixed standards of right and wrong and the conviction that Christianity was superior to all other religions.

These beliefs, however, were to be challenged throughout Europe, especially by philosophers of the day who began to communicate that God should be seen as an impersonal force, almost an energy force. It was also argued that God is not personally involved with people or with the workings of the universe.

The great debate was between the 'empiricists', who believed all helpful knowledge came from experience, and 'rationalists' who believed reason was the source of all knowledge. Meanwhile, followers of the Enlightenment – who stressed tolerance, common sense and reasonableness – saw human reason as the ultimate standard for determining truth and morals. To them, something could only be true if it could be demonstrated that it was reasonable.

Original thought at this time was directly challenged and traditional ethics based on biblical principles were seen to be outdated. Humanity was now to be the judge of right and wrong.

Self confidence in human reason was shattered by the horrors of the First World War. Human destruction was not rational or reasonable and so it was concluded that flawed human actions must be influenced by our genetic make-up or by our environment. These external forces which were outside human control meant that individuals could not be held responsible for their own actions and that life became meaningless and Godless.

The continuing story of war, economic depression and unemployment provoked people to turn to other forms of action such as political anarchy, the pursuit of pleasure and, for some, termination from a life that offered no meaningful existence.

if it feels good, do it

In this environment, existentialism flourished. The belief that truth depends upon personal experience and can be whatever you wish it to be, served a death notice upon the principle of ultimate truth. There is a willingness to respect other viewpoints and an agreement that truth is not universal but varies according to the individual. There are no set standards and no superiority of any one religion.

The three major existential philosophers are Søren Kirkegaard (1813–55), Martin Heidegger (1889–1976) and Jean-Paul Sartre (1905–80). The word 'ex-ist' means 'to stand out' and existentialist philosophers have stressed how individuals can stand out against the world, against society, institutions and ways of thought.

> **truth is subjectivity – kierkegaard** [2]

Existentialism is subjective, and concerns how people choose what they want to do and how they want to behave. Kierkegaard is referred to as the father of existentialism and stressed that 'faith begins where thinking leaves off'. He emphasised that God could only be known in an intensely personal way and therefore the truth of God is an intensely personal truth.

31

> everyone is the other and no one is himself
> – **heidegger** [3]

Heidegger emphasised human freedom and having to live and search for human values. He evaluated that because there was no God, human beings face nothing except their own extinction. He simply believed that the majority of philosophers had passed over the most important question of all – the question of 'being'. He also spoke out against the dangers of belonging to the crowd, saying that the crowd often becomes the soul of a person's life, setting limits to that person's possibilities. To be authentic means to be yourself.

> man first of all exists, encounters himself, surges up
> in the world and defines himself afterwards
> – **jean-paul sartre** [4]

Jean-Paul Sartre is the most famous existentialist. He explained that if God does not exist, then people find themselves in the situation where they exist but do not know what they are like and what they are for. Existence, therefore, precedes essence, because people look at themselves and experience 'nothingness' but must fill this nothingness with something.

other isms

> note how quickly isms become wasms
> – **richard england** [5]

There are many other influences that have shaped modern society and a few must be mentioned here.

The mass media together with increasing travel opportunities and a significant growing ethnic population have given us greater awareness of other faiths. This pluralistic outlook believes that many roads lead to God and the emphasis is upon toleration of other faiths, beliefs and ideologies.

We also live in a society where religious thinking, practice and institutions have lost social significance. This secularisation of society has caused people to question the authority of the Church and to be sceptical about religion in the face of scientific discovery. The December 1998 Gallup Survey found that 78 per cent of those questioned predicted that in the year 2025 organised religion will be less influential than it is today. This corresponds with 75 per cent believing that Britain will be less religious in twenty-five years. The Bishop of Oxford commented on these findings by remarking that he is 'convinced people will be more religious, even if outside mainstream Christianity. Sales of science books are up and sales of broadly religious books are up.' [6]

Relativism is also a popular concept, whereby things can only be judged right or wrong according to the specific situation and the individuals involved. No longer are there absolute values or truths.

People have also pursued personal pleasure above all else. This hedonistic lifestyle demands enjoyment and thrills regardless of consequences. There has also been a significant quest for materialism and wealth with an appetite that seems insatiable.

Overall these influences have led to quite a self-indulgent, self-gratifying age with emphasis upon 'doing your own thing'. This narcissistic philosophy has embedded itself into the very fabric of each individual, causing people to live life on a very subjective basis.

> **This secularisation of society has caused people to question the authority of the Church and to be sceptical about religion in the face of scientific discovery.**

a spiritual comeback

> young people are increasingly turning to ways of disciplining their lives. far too much attention has been paid to the material world they inhabit
> **– janet street porter**

Although the last century has caused people to question all principles of Christianity, seek the material, put faith in the philosophical and live according to the gospel of narcissism, there is no escaping the fact that the last two decades in particular have seen a resurgence in all things spiritual.

They have shown themselves to be incredibly 'spiritual' times, with many on a quest for faith and meaning. Almost weekly we hear new revelations from pre-millennial prophets unravelling the mysteries of the cosmos, disclosing the wisdom of gods and goddesses and bearing witness to the possibility of encountering personal guardian angels. Even the most hedonistic within humanity can now talk spiritual. Gone are the days when obvious, cringe-soaked links were needed in order to turn a conversation to spiritual matters. In this age of uncertainty, countless opportunities befall us to talk about faith.

Has the nineties overloaded people with despair and disillusionment? Are people pessimistic about survival and facing crises on all sides? There is definitely a longing for reality, honesty and a purpose to life with a noticeable interest in the afterlife, even though many have rejected organised religion. In this electronic age, access to debate, articles and information interchange on the

34

spiritual are in abundance over the Internet with sites actively promoting spiritual consciousness.

There is definitely a longing for reality, honesty and a purpose to life and a noticeable interest in the afterlife, even though many have rejected organised religion.

a tribe called quest

> so what will be the nineties legacy? there's a wanting, a need to believe in something. when you see through society's deceits, the flimsy moral constructs and useless, dated, vile goals, then what is there left to believe in? this loved-up, wised-up, messed-up, sped-up decade will leave its mark, imprint its battling ideals, its forceful tension, its cynical optimism upon the opening of the new millennium – **miranda sawyer, *the face***[7]

Relativism has not shed any light into the ethical chaos that surrounds us. Instead people have begun to look for a moral and spiritual framework upon which to live. If you empty a culture of God, it dies. The 1960s values have proved expensive – there has been personal cost, environmental cost and an emptiness of heart. The trend for meaning and purpose has become fashionable again. There is a pre-millennial restlessness and a new radical search to see the winds of change blow throughout every stratum of society. A few years ago Dr Patrick Dixon proclaimed, 'ethics will be a boom industry' – it seems that this is happening – and within this ethical search lies a deep yearning for relationships, stability, identity and justice.

A renowned Maltese architect, Richard England, writes, 'In

today's age, where the materialistic has overcome the spiritual, where despite scientific knowledge man still knows least about what matters most, man's need for contact with the Divine becomes an even more imperative and essential tool for spiritual survival.' [8] In his book, *The Spirit of Place*, England argues that places of solace should be placed in everyday living environments and habitats.

As life becomes more complex and evolved, there appears a growing desire to eliminate the non-essential and rediscover simplicity with many directing their energies towards enlightenment. Paul Gordon, a self-confessed atheist, calls for 'places for quiet contemplation for those of us who are not religious. A secular society has its own needs, not just material but spiritual of the soul in the most general sense.' [9]

Relativism has not shed any light into the ethical chaos that surrounds us.

nil points [10]

Each year the Eurovision Song Contest bursts onto our television screens with the dazzling promise that this 'momentous' competition will offer fine entertainment and great songs, interspersed only by Terry Wogan's beautifully cultivated irony. Past contests have discovered Dana, Abba, Riverdance, the stigma of 'nil points', but in 1998 something quite different was uncovered.

The hype went before her and the repercussions will continue long after she slips into obscurity – but I would suggest that Dana International (no relation to the original) won the contest not on the strength of the song but on what she represents. Everyone remembers her for being a transsexual but who can hum the tune?

Dana International sang for Israel and caused a storm. She is the embodiment of the factions that subsist within this torn and hurting promised land. She personifies the fast-growing chasm between the religious quarters and the increasing secularisation that is challenging religion to the very core.

Traditions that have survived generations are now facing possible extinction or at best dilution, as the young swop them for exciting new values and contemporary worldviews.

Fear of 'secularisation' is also being felt closer to home. The news that religion-free ceremonies for naming babies will soon become a viable alternative to church baptism, is beginning to cause significant dismay among Christians and church leaders. However, the Baby Naming Society insists its ideas 'represent a sensible step forward when church baptisms were declining in number along with weddings'. [11] These 'secular' services would abandon the traditional sprinkling with holy water and replace prayers with pledges to look after the baby. Godparents would be sponsors, church music would be replaced by popular tunes and clerics would be substituted by a registrar.

This may challenge tradition but it could be translated as a positive move by the populace to engage in symbolism that is meaningful rather than dutiful. This could perhaps be symptomatic of the realisation that for many of today's spiritual searchers, church is the last place they would go to. People are hungry for spiritual meaning but sick of empty dogma. Could it be they have found other sacred places? Why else is a spiritually searching generation bypassing these historic Christian sacraments?

People are hungry for spiritual meaning but sick of empty dogma.

a new age

> a smorgasbord of spiritual substitutes for
> christianity, all heralding our unlimited potential to
> transform ourselves and the planet so that a new
> age of peace, light and love will break forth
> **– anon**

The 'New Age' is a heavily used phrase and essentially it serves as an umbrella term embracing various beliefs, practices and influences relating to eastern religions (Buddhism, Taoism), nature religions (wicca, druidism) and the occult (channelling, psychic healing etc.).

There are multitudes of books, conferences, training centres, magazines and workshops available for those who wish to pursue a spiritual dimension to life. New found spirituality is being reflected within music, television programmes and advertising, computer games, education, business and health.

> Good evening, this is the power of Enigma
> In the next hour, we will take you with us
> Into another world
> Into the world of music, spirit and meditation
> Turn off the lights
> Take a deep breath
> Relax
> Start to move slowly
> Let the rhythm be your guiding light
>
> **enigma** [12]

Even Madonna has been quoted as saying, 'God is more like the highest state of my own consciousness – it is like calling on a power I have inside myself.'

Specialist magazines such as *Prediction, Horoscope* and *Kindred Spirit* are to be found in most good bookshops with articles on personal and planetary healing, new age tourism, astrological meditations and the like. Bookshops also contain shelves of material concerned with New Age, and many towns have their own New Age bookshop filled with all kinds of healing accessories together with books and magazines.

The magazines can point you to further involvement. Live mystic lines are available for clairvoyancy, tarot readings, dream interpretations and you can discover your own destiny by phoning for an astrological reading. Crystals, minerals and gems can be bought for healing and self-transformation and psychic festivals are advertised for most weekends all around Great Britain.

Christian clergy are increasingly being called out to exorcise ghosts, poltergeists and evil spirits because of this growing fascination with the supernatural. Madeleine Bunting comments, 'Experiments with the occult including ouija boards, tarot cards and astrology are being blamed, along with the popularity of television programmes such as *The X-Files* and factual programmes on the paranormal, for leaving people confused and vulnerable.' The Rev. Irwin-Clark, an evangelical Anglican priest, says, 'Probably a week doesn't go by without me praying for someone to have some sort of spiritual bondage removed.' [13]

> pre-millennial mass enlightenment, a culmination of meditation and new age wisdom, is taking humankind to a different plane of existence
> – *frank* magazine [14]

angels

> angels speak, they appear and reappear. they are emotional creatures. while angels may become visible by choice, our eyes are not constructed to see them ordinarily – **billy graham** [15]

Robbie Williams and U2 have sung about them, Nicolas Cage was one in the film *City of Angels* – there has always been a real fascination and preoccupation with them. There are even courses and workshops to discover angels,

> offering the opportunity to explore the angelic realms and venture into our own inner kingdoms to meet the organising and creative powers who underpin our own existence and that of the cosmos. Time is given for inner adventuring and exploring the transformative and healing potential of the angelic powers. Using breathing techniques, guided visualisation and inner dialogue we will encourage the opening of channels to the Archangels. [16]

Other courses, which have been featured on GMTV, offer the opportunity to meet your own guardian angel. Apparently the presence of white feathers indicates that you have had an encounter!

Although it is in vogue to search for angels, Christians have always had a solid belief in them and consider the Scriptures to have the lowdown. They mention their existence almost three hundred times.

> the surge of interest in healing, homeopathy, herbalism, self-awareness and cosmic attunement is a sign that people are seeking greater depth and meaning – **jonathan cainer, astrologer** [17]

the power of the paranormal

A leading authority on New Age, Marilyn Ferguson, talks about the Age of Aquarius in her book, *The Aquarian Conspiracy*. She explains that every two thousand years there is a shift in the astrological pattern which, in turn, affects the fate of our planet. Apparently, we are slipping out of the age of Pisces, represented by the fish – a sign taken by the early Church to mean faith in Jesus Christ – and moving into the age of Aquarius. This is represented by a water bearer. Through techniques such as chanting and meditation, this New Age will be one of spiritual harmony where there will be worship of Mother Earth and people will seek reconciliation with nature.

Surveys suggest that this is the age of the paranormal. A leading tabloid conducted a comprehensive survey and published the results in February 1998. It revealed that as many people believe in the paranormal – things science cannot explain – as believe in God: in both cases 63 per cent.

The survey commented,

> A few years ago anyone talking about their guardian angel might have been dismissed as a crank. Today, however, more than a quarter of the population is convinced there are angels out there. Nearly half the population believe in Heaven, with women being more convinced than men, and a quarter of us believe in re-incarnation – defined as coming back to life as another person. In recent years, there has been an unprecedented explosion in the number of people consulting psychics, seeking out faith healers, attempting to contact the dead … generally being prepared to believe the unbelievable. [18]

The debate on the paranormal is obviously one that deserves to be commented on by the Christian Church. The Rev. Dr Brian Castle,

Vice-Principal and Director of Pastoral Studies at Ripon College, Cuddesdon, Oxford, said as a response to the survey, 'The interest in spirituality seems to be increasing. Within the Church there are many different responses to this phenomenon but we should not see this as a threat but a challenge. If more people are reaching out to have their spiritual needs met, then we need to make sure we're there to respond.' [18]

Interest in mystic advice is fast becoming the healthy alternative to traditional religion and most definitely illustrates the deep searchings of the soul at a time when the majority seem disillusioned with the Church.

Even Princess Diana publicly turned her back on readily available Christian advisers or professional counsellors and instead found security under the aura of her psychic, Rita Rogers. Princess Diana was typical of the large number of people who are regularly seeking paranormal relief for the tormented soul. How tragic that people feel the Church is unable to offer suitable guidance or understanding and consider it an institution bereft of spiritual treasure. Is it possible for the Church to regain the confidence of the people?

Meanwhile, whilst the people perish, the Anglican Church is *still* discussing issues that can potentially split the whole structure. Far outweighing the controversy surrounding the ordination of women is the move towards the blessing of 'single-sex unions'. These issues are of course important, but how easily they can become the main focus and sap all energy and vision from an establishment whose first priority should be to provide sanctuary and spiritual hope to the masses. There is a real danger that in the meantime, whilst the Church looks internally to find some kind of agreement, the seekers look elsewhere. [19]

Many would already say that these seekers, in particular the wealthier classes and especially women, are looking elsewhere and are exploring the whole range of mystic alternatives with a persistence that marks a lost and hurting generation.

**Interest in mystic advice is fast becoming the healthy
alternative to traditional religion and most definitely
illustrates the deep searchings of the soul.**

making contact [19]

The latest craze roaming the planet seems to be an obsession with
destiny – a deeply curious fixation about individual and collective
fate! A glance at any cinema listing would confirm this. *Event
Horizon* follows an intergalactic mission; the *Men in Black*
heroically save earth from a giant bug; *Independence Day* and
Phenomenon take us further into the alien landscape than even
E.T. could ever have imagined; and Jodie Foster's epic *Contact*
decodes a message from space and takes us with her on a journey
to the heart of the universe! *Deep Impact* and *Armageddon* are also
examples of this fascination with fate and survival. How can we
explain this insatiable desire to explore destiny or the compulsion
to grasp a little of the mystery of eternity?

The December 1998 Gallup Poll revealed that a substantial proportion of the population, around one-third, think that humans will
have made contact with alien forms by the year 2025. About the same
proportion are optimistic that space travel will be common for the
ordinary Briton. [6]

Real world events such as the Great Eclipse, predicted to occur
just after 11 a.m. on Wednesday 11 August 1999, are not fiction
but fact, and stir up huge interest. Thousands of interested
observers, including many New Agers, gather on site to experience
a slice of history, revelling in the mystery of it all. The significance
of this total eclipse is not just in the fact of its occurrence in the
run-up to the millennium, but due to the anticipation of full
darkness on 11 August beginning at 11.11 a.m. For mystically
minded people, 1111 is a holy number and in the numerous

Internet sites devoted to the number 1111, it is a wake-up call from alien intelligences.

Similar 'planetary operations' have been followed before. The faithful rallied on 16 and 17 August 1987 at more than 350 sacred sites in order to 'synchronise the earth with the rest of the galaxy'. This harmonic convergence promised UFO sightings as well as great outpourings of extraterrestrial intelligence. There were, however, no sightings of UFOs and no landings of ETs. Another major planetary activation happened on 11 January 1992 to 'open a new door for ancient powers to be released'. [20]

What is interesting is that events like these disclose an underlying desire for peace, respect to the earth and respect for the ways of nature. Many are aligning themselves with the Mother Earth philosophy, believing the earth to be a goddess, alive and with energy. People attempt to tap into this energy and rebalance it, in order to heal the planet, seek global peace and achieve a higher consciousness.

> mankind has always had a weakness for prophecy – knowing the unknowable and thereby almost, but not quite, controlling the future – **jane kelly** [21]

How can we explain this insatiable desire to explore destiny or the compulsion to grasp a little of the mystery of eternity?

god on the box

Hollywood is reflecting this enormous quest for meaning and fascination with the supernatural. *Meet Joe Black* portrays Death walking the earth in human form and *What Dreams May Come*, explores the issues of heaven and hell. Robin Williams, who stars

44

in *What Dreams May Come*, says that the film 'triggers people's fascination with love and death'. [22] Of his own spiritual experience he comments, 'I went to this black church, people dancing, falling down and testifying and signifying. First time I saw the possibility of religious ecstasy in terms of the spirit and the music.' [22]

The Bible is full of fascinating stories and the full length animated feature film, *The Prince of Egypt*, produced by Dreamworks, although not biblically accurate, recalls the epic tale of Moses. The official film website promotes 'an epic drama that tells the story of 2 men, one born a prince, the other born a slave, but only one was born to lead'. With such a thrilling story is it any wonder that biblical epics are becoming box office hits? The numerous other websites connected to this film give Bible notes and comments about Moses and other Old Testament stories. The Internet, together with the movie industry, is successfully bringing biblical stories to a new generation who would possibly not have heard them elsewhere.

Shirley MacLaine's debut film as director, *Bruno*, is about a small boy who wants to be an angel, and *Holy Man* features Eddie Murphy playing a religious guru who becomes a frontman for a home shopping channel. Films like *The Apostle* and *Leap of Faith*, amongst countless others, also tackle the mystery and excesses of religion. Although not always positive, the conclusion is that Hollywood and beyond is responding to the felt needs within the hearts of women, men and children. But let us not forget that supplying the demands of these felt needs also guarantees profit!

Religious programming on British television seems to be undergoing a severe shift of emphasis. Historically, programmes like *Songs of Praise* have been aimed at a conventional religious audience, with very little influence from the more contemporary or alternative worship environments. As conventional religious interest has waned generally, audiences for these programmes have obviously declined. Apart from a few attempts, notably Channel 4's

45

God In the House, no effort has been made to involve the increasingly popular contemporary forms of Christian worship. Thus the BBC, in particular, have abandoned 'Christianity' for a more 'New Age' approach to faith. More attention is now given to seances and pagan practices than to dynamic Christianity.

The Heaven and Earth Show and *The Big End* are perfect examples of liberal religious programming that follow the crowd rather than lead the way. Perhaps the programme makers are oblivious to the examples of dynamic Christianity that do exist, but often the only references to anything remotely Christian are cynical. I like the approach that widens religious issues to life issues and topics of interest. I like the approach of trying something a little different, but I cannot help but despair at how 'out of touch' they are with dynamic radical Christianity that is outworked by thousands across Britain.

The Big End, a tongue-in-cheek exploration of exotic beliefs and strange spiritual groups, has even chosen a transvestite tele-evangelist to take part in the show. 'Sister Paula' Nielson describes herself as a 'transevangelist' and is a part-time hostess in a homosexual nightclub in Portland, Oregon. The Church of England are accusing the BBC of 'marginalising religion', but a BBC spokesman said, '*The Big End* is a satirical show, a different way to put across spiritual issues.' [23]

Every other faith seems to get a fair showing, when will non-religious Christianity get an opportunity?

Perhaps the programme makers are oblivious to the examples of dynamic Christianity that do exist, but often the only references to anything remotely Christian are cynical.

jesus on-line

> we stand at the start of a delicate dance of technology and faith, the marriage of god and the computer networks – **joshua cooper ramo**, *time* **magazine** [24]

The Internet is providing limitless access to spirituality, regardless of what faith or ideology the user may subscribe to.

There are chat rooms for interchanging opinions and personal beliefs, opportunities to e-mail prayers, web sites that inform the seeker of miraculous happenings around the world, worship meetings transmitted to your monitor and even the possibility for the faithful to gather electronically at their own cyberchurch. A whole host of new liturgy could potentially be introduced to provide cybercommunion, cyberworship, cyberprayer meetings and possibly even cyberbaptism where the believer is immersed in digital waves rather than water.

The Internet is an affluent provider of information and is steadily gaining a reputation for being an agent of transformation. Joshua Cooper Ramo writes,

> It is a vast cathedral of the mind, a place where ideas about God and religion can resonate, where faith can be shaped and defined by a collective spirit. Such a faith relies not on great external forces to change the world, but on what ordinary people, working as one, can create on this World Wide Web that binds all of us, Christian and Jew, Muslim and Buddhist, together. Interconnected, we may begin to find God in places we never imagined. [24]

As the search for faith continues to be high on the agenda, and as the Internet develops and widens, these two soul mates can only get closer. The only cause for concern will be when the Internet, instead of leading the user *to* God, becomes God!

> the harvest is even more bountiful on the web,
> where everyone from lutherans to tibetan buddhists
> now has a home page, many crammed with
> technological bells and whistles
> – *time* magazine [24]

the religion of science

> if a man really wants to make a million dollars,
> the best way to do it would be to start a religion
> – l. ron hubbard [25]

Hollywood celebrities have also aligned themselves with religion. The most fashionable being Scientology and the most notable members include Tom Cruise, Kirstie Alley and John Travolta. Scientologists believe that we are not merely minds and bodies but spiritual beings, temporary vessels for immortal souls called Thetans and we can become 'operating Thetans' by examining painful memories and exorcising them. This is done through intensive counselling or 'auditing' and mental pain is measured by an electropsychometer, a machine L. Ron Hubbard invented for the purpose.

The Church of Scientology claims to have eight million members worldwide and 100,000 in Britain, remarkable progress despite fervent opposition who insist it is more like a sinister cult than a religion. Hubbard's theory was that the human brain was like a computer, infinite in memory and divided into the 'analytical' and 'reactive'. Stress and pain, for example, would be recorded in the reactive mind as engrams. Dianetics was a simple technique to gain access into these engrams and move them to the analytical mind, in order to eradicate their influence. His book explaining Dianetics was soon a bestseller and turned Hubbard into a celebrity. Before long Dianetics gave way to Scientology and by 1954 the Church of Scientology was established.

Whatever the truth really is about Scientology, one cannot escape the fact that it has flourished over the last thirty years and that household names are singing its praises.

good and healthy [26]

The Christian Church is so often the subject of bad press. Most weeks we read articles that highlight the negatives and only serve to exacerbate division rather than inform us of the many positively good things that can be found within church life.

How pleasing to come across a news article entitled 'The gospel of good health'. It blissfully proclaimed, 'going to church once a week not only raises spiritual awareness, it also lowers blood pressure. According to a new study, regular churchgoers who also pray or study the Bible daily are 40 per cent less likely to have a high reading than those who don't.' [27]

David Larson, of the US National Institute for Healthcare Research summed up the findings by declaring that church attendance is better for your health. How interesting to read research that suggests this gospel of good news is also a gospel of good health.

For many years the expanding New Age movement has focused on the holistic nature of spirituality, seeking to enlighten the individual into understanding the interrelationship between mind, body and soul. This has been a strong feature of 'alternative

49

faith' and one which the media has documented and advertised with fascination. Guidebooks and technique manuals outlining holistic remedies and therapies have escalated and powerful personal testimonies have consistently featured in magazines, books, newspapers and on television. The interest in complementary medicine reveals an acceptance within the human being that life is multidimensional and that there is a union between the spiritual and the physical.

The Christian gospel has always assumed this union. Early in the Gospels you are encouraged to 'love the Lord your God with all your heart and with all your soul and with all your mind and with all your strength'. Jesus was also interested in the physical and emotional as well as the spiritual. Alternative spirituality has received the favour of the press over these past ten to fifteen years, whereas traditional or conventional Christianity has unfortunately been labelled as 'unfashionable' and not deemed newsworthy enough to be profiled.

But the gospel of Jesus is highly dynamic and supernatural. Articles such as 'the gospel of good health' are hopefully heralding a new age – one in which the miraculous Christian message will not be silent.

The interest in complementary medicine reveals an acceptance within the human being that life is multi-dimensional and that there is a union between the spiritual and the physical.

loud and clear

ever since nietzsche's astute fool, that first post-modernist, came down from the mountain and prophesied the death of god, western civilisation has tried its best to oblige. and so here we are a century later, the entire horizon sponged away. but wait. what's that sound? a small but noisy contingent are fleeing up the mountain. 'god is not dead,' they say. 'we are god.'

just ask any new age mystic or medium. the fallacy for atheist and pantheist is the same, however. both have turned inward to heal the soul. without the horizon, one can hardly blame them. what other options do they have? christianity? forget it. we christians have done such a poor job communicating that we are in part responsible for our civilisation's atheistic and pantheistic wanderings. maybe when we stop defending ourselves and start apologising to non-christians for the terrible job we have done, maybe then we will see this changed. maybe then the ultimate hope and meaning in the gospel will be returned for the world to see in the new millennium – **charles strohmer, author and philosopher** [28]

Churches caught up in the religious 'trap' of liturgy without life and weekly meetings without community, appear to be light years away from the genuine definition of following Jesus. Instead they have become nothing more than institutionalised religion.

There is an increasing sound from the thousands of people for whom Jesus is a radical lifestyle. This 'church' does not simply wait for people to visit its building, but endeavours to live out the tenets of the Christian faith at work, college, in the home, at the supermarket or down the pub! Wherever did this strange concept of 'visiting' church come from anyway? Surely church visits people, in as much as church is not the building but is a collective term for those who follow the teachings of Jesus.

With an energetic sobriety, these people are committed to live a life dedicated to Jesus. They vow to model selflessness and justice in a narcissistic and prejudiced age. Absorbed into the culture, but not obsessed by it, they are the 'I can' generation and mercifully their allegiance is to Jesus.

Gerald Coates, author and church leader, writes,

> We live in a self-mutilating culture, and what we are witnessing is not young people rebelling against the system, but the system rebelling against the very ideas and principles upon which it has been built. The result is a hurting, addicted society ready for the gospel.
>
> Attendance at Christian events has rocketed. Thousands prayer walk their towns as part of March For Jesus, 50,000 worshipped Jesus at Wembley Stadium in June 1998, and by the year 2000 several million will have been through an Alpha course introducing the gospel to the churched and un-churched.
>
> Revival has to do with such an outpouring of God's Spirit that even the unchurched know that God is in the land. [29]

---

people need to trust and they need faith. at the close of the 20th century, we are beginning to recognise the truth of g. k. chesterton's saying 'when men and women cease to believe in god, they do not believe in nothing. they believe in everything.' – **gerald coates** [29]

---

revolutionary?

> jesus created an absolute revolution in the lives of
> the people who wrote the gospels – **tom ambrose** [30]

An advertising campaign shows Jesus looking remarkably similar
to Che Guevara with words underneath saying, 'Meek, Mild, As
If. Discover the real Jesus.' This image has caused great
controversy.

Traditionalists are appalled, believing the adverts 'trivialise the
mystery of the godhead'. The revised image is diametrically
opposed to the more accepted 'sepia portrait of Jesus, happy and
smiling in dress and halo,' observes Rev. Owen-Jones, who
disagrees with the 'Saviour of the comfy slippers mentality'. One
of the 'creatives' behind the design, Chas Bayfield, adds, 'Christ is
misrepresented terribly. It's almost insulting. I want to be known
as a follower of this amazing revolutionary man, not some
effeminate fairy in a white dress.' [30]

the dome

The most controversial aspect of the much publicised and
criticised Millennium Dome has possibly been the sector featuring
aspects of faith. In the pluralistic culture of present-day Britain the
organisers have been unclear as to what to include in the sector
and vague concerning the profile of Christianity. Many have
disapproved of the dome for 'marginalising Christianity' in what
was once a Christianised society and for ignoring the central
meaning of the Millennium, the birth of Christ.

Plans to give Christianity 'pride of place' included the provision
of a resident chaplain to offer visitors spiritual guidance and

prayer in a 'church'. Strangely, in the proposed designs, this 'church' is quite separate from the spirit zone which has its own contemplation area. Although space is given to a section illustrating the life of Jesus, my only fear is that if the Christian element takes on a more 'institutionalised' feel rather than a dynamic presence, it will end up looking historic and irrelevant alongside more fashionable spiritual paths.

> **... my only fear is that if the Christian element takes on a more 'institutionalised' feel rather than a dynamic presence, it will end up looking historic and irrelevant alongside more fashionable spiritual paths.**

the census

> society is changing and people are more concerned about what they believe. faith is far more important to how they see themselves – **dr jamil sherif, muslim council of britain** [31]

The year 2001 will put faith back into religious beliefs when the official census will ask Britons to give their religion for the first time since 1851. In an ever increasing ethnic population, Home Secretary Jack Straw 'believes that people are identifying themselves in terms of their religion and culture more than ever before.' [31]

The outcome will be interesting. It appears that people are being prepared for such a timely question of faith.

Healing Waters

> many are heralding the rise to popularity of alternative medicine as the most exciting development in the medical arena for years, while others have severe reservations – **roger ellis** [1]

The whole arena of medicine and healing is high on the agenda for people living in today's world. The holistic nature of spirituality, seeking to enlighten the individual into understanding the inter-relationship between mind, body and soul, has caused people to look for this same inspiration to be at the heart of western medicine. Thus holistic health has become increasingly popular with its emphasis on the wholeness of mind, body and spirit.

Although there is huge respect and appreciation for the medical knowledge and skill within the western world, there is also a frustration. Treating the symptoms only, lack of communication, readily prescribed pills for the malaise are only a few of the reasons why people have become fascinated with the holistic approach which recognises that humanity is multidimensional and that there is union between the physical and spiritual. Alternative medicine, more aptly described as complementary medicine, is flourishing in these enlightened times.

Some medics put this massive take-up as consumer dalliance but others believe it reflects a profound cultural and philosophical shift attributed to disillusionment, with the often hurried and impersonal care delivered in medical practices. Researcher Mohammed Siahpush writes in the *Journal of Sociology*, 'There has also emerged a new value system, viewing nature as benevolent and safe, and science and technology as potentially harmful. This new philosophy is not likely to wane, on the contrary, this green culture is becoming more widespread and we can expect further growth and popularity of alternative therapies in the future.' [2]

> **Alternative medicine, more aptly described as complementary medicine, is flourishing in these enlightened times.**

mind, body and spirit

> in their search for improved health, more and more people are turning away from prescribed drugs, and are looking for a gentler alternative
> – **eileen fletcher** [3]

The official programme of the 'Festival for Mind, Body and Spirit' contains workshops on: karma healing and aura cleansing, the healing power of crystals, healing through gems, native American healing techniques, how to develop your own healing techniques plus many others. Other workshops on offer at regional New Age centres include: shamanic healing, soul therapy, healing the sacred chakra – a healing ceremony for women and self re-creation offering the individual a 'magical rebirth' and a chance to work out fears, hatreds and jealousies.

There is a plethora of imaginative and mystical workshops and techniques on offer to a world aching for holistic nourishment. Even though the titles and subject matter can sound totally unbelievable, to many it all seems thoroughly believable and definitely worth investigating.

energy levels

> the principle behind healing is tapping into a universal power, the link between the physical and the spiritual, an energy. it is about restoring the body's balance – **dr craig brown, chairman of the national federation of spiritual healers**

Holistic medicine offers a variety of therapies ranging from Acupuncture to Homeopathy and Colour Therapy to Reflexology. Many of the underlying principles of holistic medicine have derived from eastern spiritualism such as Taoism and cult practices such as dowsing.

The human body is said to have an energy flow, described as 'chi', a Chinese term, or 'ki', the Japanese term, or 'the world soul' which is the Tao term. Hindu philosophy would describe this life energy as 'prana'. The concept is as old as the mind-body healing of shamanism practised by the medicine men and witch doctors. Components of this life force or cosmic energy are the yin and yang and they circulate through a complicated system of channels called 'Meridians'.

Samuel Pfeifer MD describes these components in his book *Healing at Any Price?*

There had been speculation in ancient China about a natural force that had generated the universe. This cosmic energy was called Tao and its varied manifestations were explained by the polar forces of Yin and Yang. The two faces of Tao, Yin and Yang, are opposed to one another and yet still one. In contrast to biblical teaching, Taoism does not recognise between the opposing forces of light and darkness, God and Satan. Good and Evil come from the same source.

Chinese medicine understands man as one in body and spirit, a complete unit, finding its harmony only in Tao. The emotions, inner organs, virtues and elements are interrelated with the cosmic energy, Chi, which permeates the whole universe and man. The enlightened one, who studies the correlation between body openings and inner organs, gains comprehensive knowledge about heaven and earth.

According to Chinese theory, the Chi of the body is received from the Chi of the air. From there it enters the respiratory system which is in turn connected to the large intestine. The stomach, on the other hand, filters Chi out of the food and passes it to the spleen. Man can only function properly when his Chi is in harmony with the cosmic energy. [4]

This energy flow ensures our wellbeing and any imbalance in energy shows itself in illness and pain. Understanding the nature of this energy flow or life force helps us to understand what is at the basis of holistic complementary medicine. Therapists and healers aim to pinpoint the imbalances or disruptions to your energy flow and rebalance this energy on an emotional, spiritual or physical level, hence the holistic approach.

abundant life

> if healing does have an effect more than the placebo, we are faced with something tremendous. But at the moment most GPs remain sceptical because people are extremely gullible and the placebo effect is extremely strong
> **– professor edzard ernst, professor of complementary medicine at exeter university** [5]

Articles explaining complementary therapies and self-help techniques are to be found in abundance within national newspapers, journals and magazines. Previously hard to find material is now at the fingertips of every man, woman and child. This has obviously generated more interest but also reflects the appeal and intrigue found within humanity for the more eastern approach to life and medicine.

Television programmes, documentaries and videos have also identified the trend towards the holistic approach and more people than ever are now aware of the many therapies which exist.

A leading tabloid conducted a comprehensive survey and published the results in February 1998. Of those interviewed 40 per cent believed that some people can cure illnesses by the power of the mind, and 29 per cent believed that some people can cure illnesses by the power of God. Those studying the results concluded, 'this adds to the already powerful body of evidence that we are turning to alternative therapies.' [6]

Healing is popular in celebrity circles, the sporting world – for example Eileen Drewery's inclusion on the England World Cup Squad – and with scientists who are scrutinising this prevalent direction. The *Journal of the Royal Society of Medicine* published research which found healing to be highly effective. Apparently 81 per cent of the people in the study, all of whom had long term conditions such as arthritis and depression, reported that their symptoms had improved and they were feeling better after three months.

Healing takes many forms: some is 'hands-on' contact healing, some is done at a distance. Eleanor Bailey, in her article 'Plug in to healing power', explains, 'Some healers believe it is a gift they are born with, some that it is a gift from God, and others that it is a skill that can be taught'. [5] A worrying thought is that anyone can call themselves a healer. Currently around 14,000 practise in the UK with only half apparently trained. In order to rectify this more training courses are becoming available.

Michael O'Doherty, co-director of the healing organisation Plexus, comments, 'The potential to heal is within us all, but has been overwhelmed by our faith in western scientific values. The body has its own independent energy system which is separate from the nervous system. The energy system can become blocked and a healer re-opens the channels. We don't make people better, we prompt the body to heal itself.' [5]

> people are not content with a purely rationalistic view of the world. the wave of interest at the moment is connected to the millennium
> – james jones, bishop of liverpool [6]

Television programmes, documentaries and videos have also identified the trend towards the holistic approach and more people than ever are now aware of the many therapies that exist.

yoga

> yoga is about the alchemy of breath and movement.
> its purpose is to stretch the body, still the mind and
> open the heart – **anna pasternak** [7]

Yoga, the esoteric aerobic experience for the nineties, unites the spiritual with the mental and the physical, and is growing in popularity. Madonna has brought attention to a Slovenian yogini called Sabrina Mosek, who combines ancient prayer hand gestures, called mudras, with breathing techniques. Hand poses in the choreography for Madonna's video, *Ray of Light*, were inspired by Mosek's book on mudras.

In an interview with Anna Pasternak, Mosek explains that she 'studied ancient techniques and realised that certain poses combined with breathing can have astonishing effects. Our fingers are connected to our energy centres, which are situated all over the body. Mudras are extremely valuable ancient healing techniques that need to be revealed to the world.' [7]

When high profile and influential people like Madonna broadcast techniques such as these to the world, they suddenly take on a level of respectability. There are mudras for every occasion: for guidance, for better speech projection, for serenity and empowerment, for every mental condition and addiction, and in this present age of stress and rage, they hold a great attraction.

Yoga, the esoteric aerobic experience for the nineties, unites the spiritual with the mental and the physical, and is growing in popularity.

the alternatives

crystals

Crystals have become the ultimate New Age consumer product, easily available in many shops and with the added bonus of being a fashion item. Gems and crystals have been used for thousands of years in ancient Egypt and China, and they are said to have an individual energy field that can interact with human energy and re-balance the imbalances, clearing chakra blockages. People wear them, drink them in powder form and even sleep under them. Certain colour crystals are assigned specific chakras and a therapist can advise.

Opinions vary as to whether they do actually possess healing powers or whether they instigate the placebo effect. 'Placebo' is from the Latin meaning 'I will please' and in the Middle Ages was used to describe a fawning hypocrite. Modern medicine has adopted the term to define a medication prescribed only to please the patient, but contains no active ingredients. 'Placebos' can have great effect and it has been remarked by an expert that placebos are drugs.

colour

Colour therapists explain that each human is a 'walking rainbow' and that we carry around an 'aura'. They read this aura and advise as to which colour or colours we are lacking. Absence or lack of colour can block chakras and increasing this colour can be achieved through the environment or visualisation.

The fashion accessory world often takes a current trend and uses it as the basis for marketing a product. A company in LA has released Colour Therapy Nail Potions, bottled in fifty colours, each with its own personalised affirmations, e.g. Indara, a frosty pink: 'I am a sparkling, vibrant radiant beauty inside and out.'

acupuncture

> every needle the acupuncturist twirls between his fingers, bears the heavy weight of universal harmony in its slim pointed end – **dr duke** [8]

Acupuncture and its related therapies of acupressure, shiatsu and reflexology have their roots in ancient Chinese and Indian traditional medicine, and eastern philosophy such as Taoism. The object is to restore the energy imbalance by removing blockages through inserting needles into specifically located needling points and massage. With reflexology, the therapist searches for points in the patient's body which are unbalanced and reflected in the microsystem of the foot.

homeopathy

Homeopathy, founded by Samuel Hahnemann (1755–1843), gives the patient a remedy that will cause the same symptoms in a healthy person as those observed in the sick person. It works on the principle of curing like with like. Homeopaths use the smallest possible amount of the drug, prepared by diluting and shaking in a solution of alcohol and water. The teaching behind this asserts that shaking releases dynamic energies, believing that almost a cosmic force is transmitted in the shaking. The more the dilution, the more the potency.

Homeopathy cannot be proven scientifically and many attribute its success to the placebo effect. Although critics consider it absurd, it is very popular. Incidentally Hahnemann was influenced by eastern philosophy, Mesmer's study into hypnosis and Paracelsus who brought mystical research into medicine. The theory of curing like with like, one of the foundational tenets of homeopathy, is based upon the Law of Similarity, the second principle of magic.

natural/unnatural

The last two decades have seen a huge interest in herbal remedies. It is important to recognise that medicine has made use of natural substances and many drugs are based on plant extracts or chemical copies of plants, and herbs have provided the resource for the discovery of vital drugs used today. Herbs contain beneficial properties that can stimulate the nervous system and as well as pain relievers being derived from herbs, research into the effects of pollution and the environment is shedding new light on many diseases. In the field of nutrition, valuable work is also being done to improve health and prevent illness.

The latest wonder drug 'Pycnogenol' is derived from the bark of a Maritime Pine tree and could revolutionise treatment of heart disease and slow some effects of ageing. It is an energy-booster, working as an anti-oxidant, strengthening the immune system and comes in capsule form. Scientists say that it is fifty times more powerful than vitamin E and twenty times more powerful than vitamin C. David Derbyshire comments, 'The natural chemical Pycnogenol is five times better than traditional drugs such as aspirin at preventing the clustering of platelets in the blood – a major cause of heart disease and strokes.' [9]

Other popular pills include: 'Omnium', a deep purple multi-vitamin boasting nutrients, plant compounds and vitamins including natural beta carotene, vitamin C and minerals, and 'Pomegranate', which allegedly protects against cancer, liver damage and viral infection by killing harmful bacteria and toxins in the body. It comes as a tincture or dry rind and is now available in capsule. There will no doubt be an abundance of natural based pills introduced onto the market to cope with our ever changing lifestyle.

However, within the whole sphere of herbal remedies and essential oils, there is growing opposition to those that align the use of occult or psychic powers to herbs and oils. Aromas can quite naturally refresh and revitalise but some attach psychic experiences and magical forces to certain smells, believing that oils resonate in harmony with the spiritual aspect of the user. Similarly, cosmic powers have been assigned to herbs. Anthroposophy, founded by Rudolph Steiner, has done just this and based his medical views upon astrological influences. In contact with spirit guides, he set his goal to integrate science and religion. The Bach Flower Remedies advertise that the flowers can set free power which is the life force to heal all kinds of emotional and physical malaise, 'restore peace of mind and hope to the sick.' [10]

Critics fully support the natural properties of herbs, flowers and smells but question the validity of the psychic powers attached to them and the influences which established the basis of the remedy.

… within the whole sphere of herbal remedies and essential oils, there is growing opposition to those that align the use of occult or psychic powers to herbs and oils.

the future is integration

the public has to consider whether an investment in unproven medication is a better investment than spending more time with their GP
– mohammed siahpush, researcher [2]

Many people are using alternative therapy alongside conventional medicine, but not necessarily telling their doctor. There are obvious risks to this. However, so little research has been done by the medical establishment into alternative medicine, that it cannot informatively contradict the positive press. This situation is beginning to change and the meeting of orthodox and alternative is now being called 'integrative'.

At a UK conference for integrative medicine Iain Chalmers said,

> Critics of complementary medicine often seem to operate a double standard, being far more assiduous in their attempts to outlaw complementary medical practices than unevaluated orthodox practices. These double standards might be acceptable if orthodox medicine was based solely on practices which had been shown to do more harm than good, and if the mechanisms through which their beneficial elements had their effects were understood, but neither of these conditions apply. [2]

It is thought more than 60 per cent of orthodox treatments have not been scientifically proven and what has arisen is the need for a range of reliable tools to assess the effectiveness and safety of any health care, orthodox or complementary. An editorial in the *New England Journal of Medicine* states, 'There cannot be two kinds of medicine – conventional and alternative. There is only medicine that has been adequately tested and medicine that has not … once a treatment has been tested vigorously, it no longer matters whether it was considered alternative at the outset. If it is found to be reasonably safe and effective, it will be accepted.' [2]

Research on alternative therapies is gradually making its way into respected medical journals and pharmacists are beginning to identify traditional herbal remedies. The alternative is becoming mainstream and the pharmaceutical companies are converting this demand into currency. The integrative approach, however, still has its critics. Michael Cleary, a GP who uses homeopathic medicines much more extensively than pharmaceutical drugs, explains that the focus of orthodox medicine will continue to be misplaced. 'The problem is a philosophical one. The emphasis in orthodox medicine is on the treatment of symptoms ... alternative therapies regard a symptom as indication of some disturbance or imbalance within the person. Treating the symptom only simply moves the disturbance to somewhere else in the body. This approach may be profitable for the practitioner, but there is little in it for the patient.' [2]

> ... the meeting of orthodox and alternative is now being called 'integrative'.

the interview

Alexandra Graves is a registered Craniosacral Therapist. Craniosacral therapy is a 'hands on' therapy based on a number of findings about the body's subtle physiology, which were made by osteopaths in the US nearly a hundred years ago. Stresses, strains, tensions or traumas get 'stored' in the body and restrict functioning, giving rise to both physical and emotional effects. A therapist will, by using the hands, provide an opportunity for the body to let go of its restrictive pattern and return to an easier mode of functioning.

Why are people becoming more interested in complementary medicine? What are they looking for?

Conventional medicine is often frightening, impersonal and disempowering. Complementary medicine is often safer, more calming, slower and empowering. Even though the client may not consciously realise it, they are searching for themselves, for an awareness of who they are.

How do you see the future regarding complementary medicine?

Complementary and conventional medicine are going to have to work as a team, learning from one another. The only concern I have with this partnership is the obsessive movement towards scientifically proving complementary modalities. This need for proof beyond a doubt may narrow the infinite possibility within the complementary therapy, trying to distil the undistillable.

What are people going to need in the new century?

People will need to accept that mind and body really operate as one highly integrated system. They reflect each other completely, with the one difference that the body never lies. We need to listen to our bodies and to become intimate with our own holistic language. We must take full responsibility for our experience.

Do you believe in miraculous healing?

Yes, but I wouldn't call it miraculous. I believe we are capable of healing ourselves of anything. We have our own healing plan innately present within any disease. We never lose our health, but there has to be a balancing of different factors for healing to emerge. These factors are many and varied and depend on the individual, but awareness and trust are the foundation for this balance.

Who or what is behind the miracle?

Everything and everyone is. We are all one within this universe, we all have the same connected energy running through us. We live in a sea of this energy, within which there is infinite possibility.

a healthy mind

> open my eyes that I may see, the presence that is
> all about me
> open my ears that I may hear, the voice that is
> quiet yet ever near,
> open my heart that I may feel, the love of God close
> and real,
> open each sense, make me aware,
> of the power and peace always there.
> **david adam 'the eye of the eagle', spck** [11]

The age of western enlightenment in the eighteenth century was a time when increasing scientific knowledge gave rise to strong criticism of Christian religious beliefs. This age of reason was summed up in the thoughts of Thomas Paine, a deist who believed in an unknown, almost impersonal supreme being. He said, 'It is the duty of man to obtain all the knowledge he can and make best use of it.' [12]

John Drane, in his book *What is the New Age Saying to the Church?*, writes, 'The enlightenment dream has turned into a nightmare. But the dream will not go away. People still aspire to a better life. A life in which we can live in harmony with one another, at peace with our planet and in tune with ourselves.' [13]

It seems that the age of reason has left people pale and colourless, with the search for information and knowledge failing to satisfy spiritual yearnings. Drane continues by saying, 'In the search for ultimate answers people will as readily look to the shamans of native North American religions as to visitors from other planets. Things that were being dismissed a generation ago are now projected onto the centre stage as the key to the meaning of life's mysteries.' [14]

In contrast, the Indian understanding of enlightenment is

attained when ordinary consciousness is calmed and the 'mind-ocean finally stops at the further shore of nirvana'. Nirvana is the Buddhist word for release, liberation, an ultimate state of bliss, transcendental knowledge and power. Enlightenment can be achieved through meditation, religious ritual and by taking the necessary steps towards achieving a higher consciousness or realisation of your 'higher self'.

> you begin with a knapsack filled with twelve heavy stones. as you pass through and resolve the challenges of each gateway – money concerns, health issues, relationship problems, you release one of the stones, becoming lighter as you ascend. as your awareness ascends further up this stairway to the soul, the so-called mystical states begin to occur naturally – **dan millman, *everyday enlightenment*** [15]

This path to enlightenment leads the seeker either to a personal relationship with the Creator God of the Judeo-Christian faith, or to the cosmic life force that cannot be personalised but permeates all of the universe and is found by 'going within' until the individual becomes God. It is this latter esoteric enlightenment which is increasingly popular as we approach a third millennium.

With so much on offer, it is easy for the spiritual seeker to become spoilt for choice. Traditional Christian values have gone through a difficult period, often considered old-fashioned and dull. It is no surprise that television companies, books, magazines and national papers have paid more attention to the eclectic mix of New Age techniques, workshops and eastern philosophies on offer.

At a time when people are desiring the spiritual beyond the physical and eager to reach their full potential and worth, one must guard against being exploited by self-appointed gurus who claim divine power, promise the universe through techniques and teaching and inevitably become super rich. Unfortunately there is no spiritual watchdog committee, examining the claims that these so-called experts are making. If ever there was a time for personal integrity and wisdom, it is now.

> **If ever there was a time for personal integrity and wisdom, it is now.**

feng shui

> all the energies of your personal space are in a constant state of flux. yin and yang energies dance together continually – striving for the cosmic balance that brings harmony. yin is cool and dark and lifeless. yang is hot and bright and full of life. keep these forces in harmony within your home and you will enjoy good luck – **lillian too's *little book of feng shui*** [16]

Feng Shui has been very successful in translating the eastern philosophy behind the majority of alternative medicine into other areas of life. Lillian Too, author of the international bestseller *The Complete Guide To Feng Shui*, describes Feng Shui as 'Understanding the flow of chi, the hidden breath that permeates the environment.' [16]

Particular emphasis is given to the environment which you inhabit – for example within the house or workplace, shopping mall or club. Multinational companies are even calling on the gifts of Feng Shui experts to advise on interior design in order to improve the wellbeing and productivity of their workers. Design advice, according to Too, includes: regular shapes are better than irregular shapes, the ratio of windows to doors in all your rooms should not exceed 3:1 otherwise too many windows apparently causes your luck to seep away, place your bed in the corner of the bedroom diagonally opposite the entrance and never sleep with your head or feet pointing directly at the door; keep the lid down on your toilet at all times and keep toilet doors permanently shut. Tips are also given as to colour schemes, mirrors, paintings, plants, doors: the list is endless.

It seems an obvious progression for the philosophy of chi to be extended into other areas of life. Cookery books using the principles of Feng Shui are being introduced, and humorous options like Feng Shui for dogs or cats. Something so fashionable and increasing in popularity is bound to be adopted by all kinds of people and industries. Critics of Feng Shui say that obvious interior design principles have been spiritualised for a spiritual age and that it is resulting in good profit rather than good luck. However, not many people would turn down the prospect of fame, wealth, health, love and happiness unless they either see through the hype or have their own spiritual principles that conflict with the underlying ancient Chinese ethos of yin and yang.

> **Critics of Feng Shui say that obvious interior design principles have been spiritualised for a spiritual age and that it is resulting in good profit rather than good luck.**

christian healing

> is any one of you sick? he should call the elders of the church to pray over him and anoint him with oil in the name of the lord — **james 5:14, the bible, niv version**

There is a rapidly growing number of people who are followers of Jesus Christ and believe that the God of the Christian Bible designed and created the miracle of human life. The incredible intricacies of the anatomical, emotional and spiritual body are thought to have originated from God and so therefore if there is dis-ease, many believe in pursuing the power of prayer for healing. The source of healing is not in a person, or the healer, but in God.

the interview

I posed a few questions about Christian healing to Martin Scott, who has two degrees in theology, and travels in the UK and further afield teaching on prayer and encouraging the Church to be active in the healing ministry.

Why are so many people looking to alternative medicine and healing?

There are at least two main perspectives on this. Firstly, the simple one is that people are now more ready to try something that they cannot understand. We are all more open to there being realities which we cannot explain, so if something seems to work, many people are ready to give it a try. The second aspect is that there is a growing spirituality. Our world is not the ancient world of myth and legend, but neither is it the world where science rules. It is the world where spirituality is being given a greater profile and credence. And as most alternative healing embraces a spiritual dimension it is finding a place in our society.

Is the holistic approach (mind, body and spirit) compatible with Christianity?

Most certainly. The Christian (and Jewish) world view is one where

73

spiritual realities impact on the material world. If a person is sick, spiritually or emotionally, this will almost certainly have a bearing on a person's physical wellbeing. So for example, in the healings of Jesus there are a number of occasions where he forgave sin before he healed physically. Although Jesus did not suggest that people were sick because they had sinned he did indicate that there was often a connection between the two.

Are people becoming as interested in Christian healing as they are in psychic healing?

I find that very hard to answer as I have no statistics to draw on. All I can say is that there seems to be an increase in Christian churches that are seeking to practise healing, and there never seems to be a lack of people to pray for! Perhaps the difference between Christian healing and psychic healing is that Christian healing is more tied up with the Christian message, while psychic healing might be more connected to direct claims to possess psychic powers.

> christian healing is perhaps more tied up with the christian message, while psychic healing might be more connected to direct claims to possess psychic powers — **martin scott**

Do you see dangers in psychic healing? What are they?

I think that there might well be some dangers in pursuing psychic healing. Christian healing is simply asking, through prayer, for God to heal. There is no desire to tap into any inner powers, or through any particular techniques to come into contact with some universal energy. It is always hard to be dogmatic but it seems to me that there are also powers that are malevolent so caution needs to be exercised.

What are your beliefs about the power of prayer for healing?

Genuine, honest, heartfelt prayer has always been encouraged by the Church. Such prayer puts us in touch with a God who cares and loves to communicate his care in a variety of ways. I wish that prayer guaranteed healing but this is not the case. However, even when healing does not result there is a communication of the presence and love of God that comes through prayer.

Do you know of any genuine God-healings? Describe one or two.

Perhaps the most dramatic healing that I ever witnessed was of a lady called Edith. She had been diagnosed with multiple sclerosis and for the previous nineteen years had never walked unaided. She had been in a wheelchair for the last sixteen of those nineteen years. When I met her, her eyesight and voice had all but gone. She was hoping for an improvement in her voice but within days was walking, free of pain. She eventually received her driver's licence back and is now living a totally normal life again – quite often sharing her story of healing with numerous groups of people.

Then there was the young girl, called Lucy, who was brought to my office for prayer by her mother. She had been seriously ill for around three years. Initially she was diagnosed with Henoch Schonlen disease, but this had resulted in a number of different conditions. For three years she had been treated without any success, but the moment she was prayed for began to feel incredibly improved. This was confirmed by her routine blood pressure check which was normal for the first time in those three years. Within a short while she was discharged by her doctors with the statement that this was a 'miraculous recovery'. However, they apparently meant by this that the cumulative effect of three years of medication was an overnight recovery – although none had been forthcoming over those previous three years!

Is there a greater interest now in healing meetings than twenty years ago?

I think there is a greater interest in healing meetings, but also a greater interest in spiritual matters. There is a greater openness to the super-natural, which I think is good, although this could also mean that people are open to experimenting without setting any boundaries. Overall that is good but there might be some dangers that could be incurred.

What is your perspective on Eileen Drewery and what she offered the England Team?

It is always dangerous to comment on someone you have never met. I am sure she is a sincere lady and offered the hope of healing and also giving them a listening ear. Most people need someone who will give them time and attention. Perhaps, with the pressure that many GPs are under, that is another reason why people are turning to alternative practices. As a Christian I would always want to raise a question over anyone who promises healing in a way that either contradicts or goes beyond the Bible.

Is being healed a question of personal faith?

There is often faith involved in healing. Even at the level of going to the doctor there is often faith exercised. If someone is convinced they will not get better then it seems to be that they often do not recover. I have also found that there are occasions when people are healed who never expected it. There do not seem to be 'rules' that apply but where there is no expectation at all then healing is unlikely to take place.

The Sexual Explosion I

everybody's doing it ![1]

> you hear about it all the time – on television and in books and you think 'that looks good'. you want to try it because it's a new experience. if something looks really good you want to do it – **'what 14 year olds say about sex' survey**

'Do you realise what you've just done?' I remarked boldly. The face of the sales assistant seemed devoid of interest. 'You've just sold that magazine to an eleven-year-old and the front cover explicitly states, *"Not to be sold to anyone under 18".*' I was clearly wasting my time. This shop assistant, like many others, chose the sale rather than the ethic.

This is only one example of unsuitable material read by children and teenagers – at least a warning was displayed. The real culprits are the 'soft-porn' handbooks of sexual experimentation and promiscuity that masquerade as 'teenage magazines'.

A cursory glance at a particular batch reveals a true life story of a girl who slept with forty boys in three months; a pull-out guide to 'sexpertise'; a pictorial catalogue of sex accessories and a centrefold of naked celebrities with tomato sauce bottles in strategic places! Content such as this is not sparse. Articles like these (and worse) litter the pages and transmit a constant diet of sleazy-messages that 'everybody's doing it', losing your virginity is an essential part of being young and sexual experiences enhance your street cred!

Bombarded by this provocation, is it any wonder that many embark on a journey of sexual adventure with tragic consequences? A 1994 survey revealed that every day in Britain: at least twenty-seven schoolgirls become pregnant, two under the age of thirteen; at least 170 babies are born to teenage mothers and at least one in three under-fourteens admit to regular sexual intercourse. It would be naive not to recognise other causal factors, but surely this constancy and quantity of visual and verbal stimuli does affect behaviour. If this axiom of human response was not true, the advertising industry would go bankrupt overnight!

Even more worrying are the recent statistics concerning under-age pregnancies with figures revealing an 11 per cent rise. Almost one in every 100 girls of fifteen or under fell pregnant before reaching the legal age for sex. More than half had abortions. [2]

Concern about these magazines is not new. To quieten a recent 'censorial storm', the Periodical Publishers' Association formulated a code of practice detailing suitability of material according to age and the Teenage Magazine Arbitration Panel began monitoring the outworking of this code. Unfortunately, nothing seems to have changed and certain 'teenage' magazines with a substantial under-age readership, continue to be as obsessed with sex as ever.

In an age where young people are voluntarily searching for moral guidance, how can we sit back and allow these 'publishing gurus' to rape today's rising generation of all dignity and value?

The content and message within these magazines are only part of the sexual explosion. Before we take a deeper look at other influences upon the libido of the nation and the impact of those influences, let us examine the sexual journey so far. By under-standing some of the history, we can speculate as to the future of sexual behaviour, with some interesting trends already taking shape.

> **Bombarded by this provocation, is it any wonder that many embark on a journey of sexual adventure with tragic consequences?**

a little history

> before we can make sense of the rapid reversals taking place in sexual relationships today, we need to look back on the last 300 years, and the three swings of the pendulum: from relaxation to restraint and then back to relaxation: but now swinging back to restraint again – **dr patrick dixon** [3]

Dr Patrick Dixon, in his book *The Rising Price of Love*, looks back over the last three hundred years. He writes,

> In the early eighteenth century, sexual freedom was tolerated and sex was certainly on the agenda. Then came a growing unease about the cost of sexual freedom as the effects of a massive spiritual awakening took a grip on the nation, starting with Wesley in the mid-eighteenth century and crusading on throughout the nineteenth. Great reformers like Wilberforce, who abolished slavery, or Lord Shaftesbury, who abolished child labour, were just part of a massive movement that championed change. As thousands discovered Christ, a new moral code swept through Britain. [4]

The Victorian era is known for its emphasis on restraint and modesty. An eminent surgeon, Dr William Acton, came to the fore and according to Simon Andreae in *Anatomy of Desire* announced, 'Women, if they had a sex drive at all, would keep it well hidden and infrequently indulged.' This 'passive' model proposed that the majority of women 'are not much troubled by sexual feelings of any kind'. [5]

This Victorian sexual suppression is challenged by Michael Mason in *The Making of Victorian Sexual Attitudes*. [6] He says that Victorian sexual repression is a myth with between a third and half of women pregnant at marriage and 'unbridled sexual intercourse' taking place in working-class dance halls. Mason also claims that Victorians were fully aware of female sexuality, opposing Acton's theory about passivity. Interesting but not surprising is that all the theorising about female sexuality was done by men, whose views revealed more about the male species and their hopes and thoughts, than they did about women. By the turn of the century women started battling to become physicians and writers themselves.

It is well documented that writer Marian Evans, aka George Eliot, was tremendously courageous as a single woman in Victorian times, and managed to strike out on her own. Through hard work she became a literary artist and one of the highest earning women in Britain, sexually liberated but interestingly not a champion of women's rights.

Regardless of the contradictory perceptions about the Victorian age, the overwhelming memory is one of temperance and reserve, although no doubt there were excesses. Dixon writes, 'The Victorians reacted against the previous century's sexual abandonment with a radical sexual revolution.' [7]

Bruce Anderson, in his essay 'Just what can Britain learn from the past?', remarks, 'a moral revival will not work unless practical measures are taken. History teaches us this can be done: it was achieved with remarkable results in late Victorian Britain. This new morality was reflected in other ways within the infrastructure of society. The prison population fell, as did the average length of sentences.' [8]

> victorian society was an enormous nexus of
> churches, voluntary organisations, and self-help
> groups which believed in a unified morality
> – **bruce anderson** [8]

the 20th century

> one destructive myth in our lives is that sexual
> activity is natural while sexual inactivity is not
> – **celia hadden**, *the limits of sex*

The First World War, 1914–18, began to change the whole culture of the nation. As the men marched off to war, the women began to have significant input into processes that were once firmly in the control of men. Women in the workplace, family roles, votes for women, a change in clothing and length of hair for women ... 'rumblings of discontent at these reductive, male orientated, rather Gothic views began to be heard', remarks Andreae. [9]

Meanwhile, historic advances were being made regarding sexual diseases and the technology of birth control. By 1905, the microbes responsible for gonorrhoea, soft chancre and syphilis had all been found and fifty years later, following the discovery of penicillin, they could also be cured. Also, in the 1920s condoms could be mass produced and easily obtained by an enthusiastic public. Prior to this, condoms had been handmade – very time consuming in construction and possibly not that reliable.

Then in 1960 came the 'mother of all birth control' – the Pill. 'It was discreet, reliable, and it offered women the knowledge that they had round-the-clock, round-the-month protection, allowing them to engage in spontaneous bouts of passion without the need to stop, blush, and ask (or face) a barrage of questions', quotes Andreae. [10] Women could now enjoy and experience freedom and assert new found control over their sexual behaviour without the pressure of an unwanted pregnancy.

> women had been under the authority of men, their fertility closely monitored and their activities curtailed and confined. all sorts of myths had been invented to sustain this situation. they were evil temptresses who must be resisted; agents of chaos who must be subdued; inferior beings who should be ignored; weaker vessels who deserved indulgence; or airy simpletons who should be troubled by nothing but frippery – **simon andreae** [10]

a sexual revolution

> the decline began, not only in our morality but our common sense. in the sixties there was a belief that sexual abandon was the way to utopia, that all restraints should be torn aside. this was a myth … promiscuity is destructive not emancipating, sex without emotion debases both men and women. we began to worship the false god of freedom – **lynda lee-potter** [11]

In their book, *Human Sexual Response*, William Masters and Virginia Johnson published the results of a detailed examination into female sexuality. [12] The year was 1967 and the effect was radical. Although changing, the legacy of female sexuality was that women were very different to men and had very little sex drive to speak of. Coupled with this, women were still seen to be inferior in all things sexual, with the male still very much the testosterone hero of orgasmic pleasure. Masters and Johnson were able to provide an account of the female orgasm, and also described what happens to men and women during intercourse. More recently they have remarked that in the 1960s and 1970s, 'There was a rush to make sex recreational, to make it fun and games, and ignoring the things that make sexual responses occur, things that deepen a relationship, that give it colour and endurance.' [13]

The Divorce Reform Act was passed in 1969 and much had changed since the assumption that only death can separate the marriage bond and according to Joan Smith in her book, *Different for Girls*, 'The number of divorces in Britain has risen inexorably from an insignificant 6,092 in 1938 to an annual figure of 158,200 in 1994.' [14]

At a time when women were exploring equality and liberation, when technology promised the possibility of risk-free sex and when society was increasingly choosing the secular way rather than the religious, a shift in cultural and sexual attitudes ushered in the now infamous Sexual Revolution.

After the end of the Second World War, sexual liberation was observed on a world-wide level. In Britain in particular, the 'Swinging Sixties' were notorious for being a time of experimentation and people courageously began to speak out for freedom and liberation. There was no stopping this self-appointed group of warriors who chose to abandon the familiar framework of behaviour and belief and treat their bodies and their spirits like adventure playgrounds.

> you would have to be a hermit to avoid the sexually arousing stimuli of contemporary culture. that which god created for enjoyment and intimacy has become perverted – **gary collins, *christian counselling***

There was no stopping this self-appointed group of warriors who chose to abandon the familiar framework of behaviour and belief and treat their bodies and their spirits like adventure playgrounds.

sex mad world – myth or reality?

> the british spend nearly 200 million every year on the sex industry. sex is so profitable, we use it to peddle anything: merchandise, love, people. we even kill for it – **jenne liburd, 'are you soft on porn?'** [15]

A preoccupation with sex and an indulgence in erotica seem to be everywhere – in the media, in the movies, in magazines, in music, in advertising, in art … The modern-day proverb has been 'the more sexually experienced you are, the more street-cred you have'. With a world view that popularises that there are now no rights or wrongs, and with rules of conduct considered to be old-fashioned in these supposedly enlightened times, people are encouraged to do whatever pleases. Every boundary appears to have been crossed, every sexual position has been illustrated and re-enacted in teenage magazine supplements and every taboo has been de-stigmatised.

music and movies

> in the 1950s elvis presley's gyrating hips were banned from american tv screens because outraged parents believed they would prove too sexually stimulating for their innocent daughters
> **– steve chalke and nick page** [16]

Music is a powerful language of communication. With the ability to entertain and educate, there is no doubt that song lyrics and artists can influence people's thinking and behaviour. Ever since The Beatles erupted onto the scene influencing whole generations, plenty more have caused mass hysteria. David Cassidy, Marc Bolan, Donny Osmond, Michael Jackson, Take That, Oasis, Madonna, Boyzone are just a few.

Regardless of whether you like the musical style, a strong message of sex without commitment and experimentation without frontiers is preached from the jukebox. George Michael, for example, sings about getting quick, easy sex and then trivialises his arrest for lewd behaviour in a Los Angeles toilet with 'Outside'. On a television chat show he maintained that he did what everyone else would do when faced with sexual temptation – go for it. The audience spontaneously applauded this declaration of promiscuity without even a word of altercation from the interviewer! Prince records a woman reaching a sexual climax on a track from his album 'Come' whilst Madonna requests some 'erotic, put your hands all over my body'. The bump 'n' grind stimuli endlessly promises 'I've got a little something for you' because 'I'm horny, horny, horny, horny'. And how can we resist the 'I wanna sex you up' offer from Colour Me Badd?

It is also commonplace to see naked or semi-naked images within music videos. Alanis Morissette's video to the song 'Thank U' has her starkers in a supermarket whilst George Michael's videos are packed with half-clad men and women gyrating in overtly sexual ways. With images based on sadomasochism, the video to Scary Spice Mel B's first foray into solo success contained a certain brand of 'girl power' that her ten-year-old fans should avoid.

Fed on a continual diet of sexual stimulation and racy videos advertising and illustrating the songs, it is claimed that people, especially younger children and teenagers who are impressionable, whilst formulating their own framework for life and behaviour, are influenced to throw aside sensible standards of morality and adopt an experimental approach.

The movie world also covers sex, relationships and sexual deviations. The larger percentage of sexual liaisons occur outside the marriage covenant, thus conveying how little the marriage agreement means and how easily it can be broken. *Crash* was said to be 'perverted and sexually deviant, advocating that orgasm can and should be generated by reckless driving and that bodily injury can be a come-on'. *The People vs Larry Flynt* almost legitimised the story of a porn baron, drug addict and convicted pimp who was made into a Hollywood hero. His wealth was built on publishing pictures of naked women, some displayed in rape fantasies and smeared in excrement. *Showgirls* featured more nudity than any previous Hollywood film.

A quick tour around your video store will reveal the vast amount of steamy, licentious films that have been made and watched. I would not want to go back to the days when married couples had to wear wincyette pyjamas from head to toe and to film the bedroom scene meant that one of them had to always keep one foot on the floor – however, many are strongly objecting to the libidinous and carnal overload dulling our senses.

> the moral well-being of the nation should be the concern of everyone – **anon**

Regardless of whether you like the musical style, a strong message of sex without commitment and experimentation without frontiers is preached from the jukebox.

television and advertising

> in western countries, kids are sent mixed messages by the media. they're told that early sexual initiation is bad, but are bombarded with images of teenagers as sexual toys. klein and most designers have used half-dressed, pouting teenagers to sell their clothes for years. society sexualises children — and then tells them sex is bad — **anouk ride, another planet** [17]

Programmes on television also convince me that we are surrounded by sex and sexual pressures. For example, *Have Your Cake and Eat It* glamorised adultery; *The Girlie Show* included everything that was sordid and exploitative; *Eurotrash* proudly showcased global pervertedness, and the increasing number of pornographic programmes on cable and satellite reduces the most precious acts of love to mere titillation and indulgence with no real basis of love and respect between the 'consenting' parties. Documentaries that follow the Brits abroad are full of the most obscene behaviour imaginable.

Sex and the City on Channel 4 has provoked hot reaction. The central character is Carrie Bradshaw and the actress who plays her explains that the show is 'basically about mating rituals in New York and how sexual relationships affect those'. [18] One episode profiles a couple having problems with anal sex.

Live TV, for example, transmits programmes containing

livecam shots of a woman (or women) in the privacy of her own bedroom exploring her own body (and each other's). Surely this is voyeurism at its worst, but marks the trend of television to be more daring than ever and highlights the need for sufficient censorship to be introduced.

The number of advertisers who use sex to sell a product has increased. It sells cars, ice cream, chocolate, drink – the list is endless. We are promised that if we buy that 'certain' product then our chances of finding a mate will suddenly increase. The Impulse advert always amuses me. Walking down the street wearing Impulse apparently guarantees you a man jumping out at you with a large bouquet of flowers. In reality, if that happened, you would more than likely be tempted to hit him and call the police, than entertain his romantic advances!

Many people feel that using sex to sell a product cheapens this most intimate act. It more often depicts sexual temptation and activity outside of any long-term relationship.

magazine madness

> women's bodies are treated as though human beings have no more right to privacy or dignity than a strung-up, plucked chicken. they are for the sick, the depraved, the immature – those who think sex has nothing to do with love or even affection
> – lynda lee-potter [11]

We have already looked at the state of the nation's teenage magazines in the opening section of this chapter. The content of the articles and pull-out guides is very explicit: some outline the best sexual positions and others give guidance as to how to reach the best orgasm; some give advice on the erogenous zones of the opposite sex and others describe the thrills and spills of sex in public. Mary Kenny remarks,

> Teenagers live in a world of shrieking videos and lurid magazines which advertise telephone lines for 'Oral Sex – How To Do It' and which run features entitled 'Me and My Willy'. Since adults in their droves are attracted to magazine material which markets sex relentlessly, what right have we to be surprised or moralistic about the same formula applied to the teen market. [19]

There are also lurid adult magazines on sale at high street shops. Instead of being tucked away, they are still on show and people are still calling for magazines such as *Penthouse* and *Playboy* to be censored.

Women's magazines also contain a large amount of material based around sex. Front covers promise 'Hotter than ever sex', 'Love, lust and temptation', 'Illicit sex', and 'Ultimate delicious sex'. Joyce Hopkirk, once editor of *Cosmopolitan*, explains,

> In the Seventies I was proud to be part of the movement that changed things and helped women find equality in all facets of life, including the bedroom. We adopted the slogan, 'Women can have everything'. Obviously taking charge of your sex life was part of it. But we never encouraged casual sex, we preached the opposite: do not be a victim, do not be used. Now the message is simply about sex. [20]

Recently, a national newspaper described an occasion when a woman subtly breastfeeding her baby in public caused such a negative public reaction, she was ejected from a public place. The dichotomy in society is that it is acceptable to publish pictures of

89

women's breasts on page three of the *Sun* and satisfy erotic hunger, but it certainly is not acceptable to carefully reveal a woman's breasts to satisfy a baby's hunger. A natural and beautiful bodywork between mother and baby is reduced to an infantile understanding of what is offensive and what is not. Could this be the result of the constant sexualisation of the female body due to centuries of male ownership of women?

> **The dichotomy in society is that it is acceptable to publish pictures of women's breasts on page three of the *Sun* and satisfy erotic hunger, but certainly not acceptable to carefully reveal a woman's breasts to satisfy a baby's hunger.**

red hot and blue

> pornography = explicit presentation of sexual activity in literature or films etc. to stimulate erotic rather than aesthetic feelings
> – *the oxford dictionary*

The word 'pornography' originates from two Greek words: *porne* meaning prostitution and *graphein* meaning to write, and developed from people writing about pornography. The *Dictionary of Ethics, Theology and Society* defines pornography as 'that which deals with sex or sexual activity and appeals to prurient interests or that which is obscene'. The word was only really used from the 1800s when any kind of written or visual image of a sexually explicit nature was considered pornographic. [21]

There is no law against pornography but there is a law against obscenity, and a jury is asked to decide whether the material is likely to deprave and corrupt a reasonable person. If 'yes', then the producers of the material can be prosecuted. Britain has a reputation for having the toughest stance on porn in Europe, and although women's bodies can be uncovered, it is considered obscene to show an erect penis. Approximately six per cent of purchasers of 'top shelf' porn are women and that figure is rising. Female defenders of pornography argue that if the law was changed, then porn could be produced to appeal to both sexes rather than simply appeal to a masculine society.

In order to change the status quo, the production of pornography will fall more into the hands of women than ever. Lucy Williams, who creates collages, says of her work, 'Pornography never presents the female form as something to respect and celebrate. Through my collages, I aim to present both. I want to portray the power of female sexuality by subverting offensive male representations of women and producing strong, unashamed portraits.' [15]

Steve Chalke and Nick Page in their book, *Sex Matters*, describe pornography as something which devalues men and women and turns them into sex objects. This does not mean that all nude pictures or sex scenes are pornographic – even the Bible contains a poem that is sexually explicit. The difference between pornographic and non-pornographic images is that the former are more concerned with the picture or sex act than with the story or the person. Pornography supplies you with something you want and makes sex an item for sale.

There have been studies carried out which have attempted to discover the effects of pornography. By exposing one group of people to explicit pornographic material and comparing their behavioural changes with a group that had not been exposed to the material, they found that the material lead people to become more violent and less satisfied with their partners. They were also less sympathetic to rape victims and had less desire to punish the rapist. Ted Bundy, an American serial killer who raped and murdered twenty-four women, admitted to being influenced by the violent sexual images he exposed himself to.

In 'Are you soft on porn?' Jenne Liburd reveals, 'According to Kinsey, there is very little physiological difference between an angry man and a sexually aroused one, bar certain vasodilations, orgasm and erection. Both emotions evolve from the same physiological place. It is not surprising that many frustrating sexual experiences can very easily lead to violence.' [15]

> porn is the propaganda organ of a sexist society. it's a systematic form of putting women down for men's entertainment. it's not a moral issue, it's a human rights issue – **anne mayne, campaign against pornography** [22]

In a world obsessed with sex, the boundaries of what is explicit are constantly being pushed back. More and more writers and artists are having to think of newer and more risqué ways to shock an almost unshockable audience.

Take, for example, the storm that surrounded the novel *The End of Alice*, describing in pornographic detail the physical and sexual abuse of a young girl by an unrepentant paedophile. After a long period of abuse, she is to be mutilated and killed. The chief executive of the NSPCC at that time, Jim Harding, commented, 'the book describes abuse but does not condemn it. It operates in a moral vacuum. Yet if ever there was an area in which a moral vacuum should not exist, it is child abuse. It promotes the ultimate paedophile fantasy.' [23]

Harding continued, 'Why would anyone make entertainment out of the evil workings of a demented creature determined to use a child for his personal gratification?' We have a long history of artistic freedom but this book was not educational or biographical but salacious. Many called for it to be banned as 'child abuse is too serious a subject to be treated as entertainment'. [23]

> soft porn trivialises women, hard porn trivialises sex. surround yourself with enough filth and you get immune to it – **select** [22]

> even the staunchest supporters of porn would have to concede that porn is born of a culture that tells us women are inferior and that submission and domination are erotic – **jenne liburd** [15]

cyberporn

> on-line erotica ... it's popular, pervasive and surprisingly perverse – **philip elmer-dewitt, *time* magazine** [24]

The Internet is one of the most efficient carriers of pornography and one of the most difficult to control. Thousands log onto web sites containing all kinds of sexual activity and it is a well known source for downloading pictures of sex acts involving children. Elmer-Dewitt in *Time* magazine comments, 'Pornography's appeal is surprisingly elusive. It plays as much on fear, anxiety, curiosity and taboo as on genuine eroticism.' [24]

An eighteen-month study of on-line porn by researchers at Carnegie Mellon University in Pittsburgh discovered that there was a lot of it and it was immensely popular. The researchers found 917,410 sexually explicit pictures, short stories and film clips and concluded that sexual imagery is now 'one of the largest (if not the largest) recreational applications for users of computer networks'. [24]

It is a big moneyspinner with millions lining the pockets of bulletin board systems (bbs). Research also said it was a 'guy thing'. Apparently men make up 98 per cent of the on-line users. The material is also eclectic – not simply pictures of naked women but paedophilia, hebaphilia (youths), and paraphilia (a descriptive word used for the mixed bag of deviant materials including bondage, sadomasochism, defecation and sex acts with animals).

Alarmingly, material like this is available worldwide to men, women and children and there are legitimate concerns as to the censoring of such sites. The researchers observed, however, that they 'found nothing that can't be found in speciality magazines or adult bookstores', [24] but the ability to transfer them into your home or office, school or college is extremely disturbing. Particularly disturbing when you consider that most of the Internet experts are children and teenagers and in this age of family breakdown it is not practical to leave censorship up to the parents.

There will always be those who believe 'cyberspace is a safe place in which to explore the forbidden and the taboo' [24] and opponents of censoring sexually explicit material believe that if you don't want it, you will not get it. Alternatively many feel that cyberporn presents a temptation which will become addictive and dangerous, creating an insatiable appetite. Software tools will prevent the worst abuses but there will never be a solution which will eradicate it completely because the Internet is about freedom of speech and democracy.

… cyberporn presents a temptation which will become addictive and dangerous, creating an insatiable appetite.

sensation

Take, for example, the Royal Academy's controversial exhibition 'Sensation'. Anthony Daniels, critic, recounts,

> You are met by a 14-foot Tiger Shark, slightly shabby, suspended in formalin. In the same room is a self-portrait, skilfully sculpted from eight pints of the artist's frozen blood. A room or two further on, you meet parts of two cows in thick slices, also suspended in formalin. It is like being in a pathology museum. [25]

The Royal Academy, in its wisdom, decided to include a huge portrait of Myra Hindley painted by using the palm-prints of a small child. The expertise of the artist is without question … but its inclusion within a public exhibition is an invidious display of artistic freedom and expression. Daniels comments of his 'physical sense of revulsion using a face of a woman known to the world only because she brutally tortured and then murdered several children'.[25] Defending the Academy, Norman Rosenthal believes 'art has no morality' and is happy to promote a gallery overflowing with shocking images of an amoral nature.

I was reassured by the response of the public to this framed obscenity. The normalisation of indecency which has been penetrating our human psyche is beginning to wane and with one voice united, people are saying 'enough is enough'. It was once quoted, 'True revolutions in art restore more than they destroy.' This modern form of art may unintentionally serve to destroy itself because it has totally misjudged the conscience of the nation. Art may well communicate the nature of humankind but some aspects are surely best left unsaid.

> The normalisation of indecency which has been
> penetrating our human psyche is beginning to wane and
> with one voice united, people are saying 'enough is
> enough'.

people power

> a characteristic of the nineties degeneracy is to be
> 'non-judgemental'. to be judgemental i.e. to insist
> on the difference between right and wrong, is the
> cardinal sin among the decadents — the only sin
> they recognise. they do not regard anything as
> immoral except interference with artistic expression.
> where will it end? — **paul johnson** [26]

Effective censorship has become a casualty of this post-modern
war of moral readjustment. However, people are fed up of the
relentless stream of clever platitudes justifying acts of gross
indecency. In the film *Lolita*, Jeremy Irons plays a middle-aged
paedophile who seduces his twelve-year-old stepdaughter.
Amazingly it found a British distributor, but one film critic
remarked, 'He has made a film so morally repellent that it will
tempt many a nation to toughen up its stance on censorship.' [27]
Evil triumphs when good men and women do nothing. Positive
and collective action such as boycotting the film or writing
sensible letters of complaint is essential.

Recent research by the Broadcasting Standards Committee has
found, 'There is only so much sex a person can take and it appears
that limit has been reached, and viewers' tolerance is ebbing fast.' [28]
There is an apparent increase in the past year, from 32 to 36 per cent,
in the numbers believing there is too much sex on British screens.

> censorship is a necessary part of a civilised society
> – anne atkins [29]

Pornography in the public world, pornography in the private world: the issues are far more complex than it is possible to cover in this book. One can also argue that there is a morally significant difference between pornography used for the titillation of an individual and pornography used as an aid to develop and assist a married couple's sex life. The purchase of the latter seems to offend no one and opinion often says that in a democratic country the role of the censor should be in the hands of the individual. Whatever moral stand an individual takes, the trend has definitely been towards pushing back the barriers. One hundred years ago, the conviction and imprisonment of Oscar Wilde, the paedophile, brought the end of 'a fashionable degeneracy'. Paul Johnson wonders whether the 'decadent Nineties will end with an evil elite taking charge of our culture? Or will the approach to the millennium produce a backlash even more powerful than the one that destroyed Oscar Wilde a century ago?' [26]

People are beginning to take the opportunity to influence and to contribute to the moral environment. If we fail to take or make these opportunities then we inherit the world we deserve whilst choking on our own passivity. It appears that the power of the people is finding its voice!

People are beginning to take the opportunity to influence and to contribute to the moral environment. If we fail to take or make these opportunities then we inherit the world we deserve whilst choking on our own passivity.

The Sexual Explosion II

where have all the children gone? [1]

> total freedom has not led to total happiness
> — simon andreae [2]

When BBC's *Watchdog* revealed that Walkers had been steadily reducing the weight of an average packet of their most loved crisps, the nation created an uproar and put the blame firmly at Gary Lineker's feet, purporting that his appearance fees had forced Walkers to take cost-cutting measures. However, there is a greater and more disastrous loss happening before our eyes.

Recent statistics reveal that more than one in ten girls aged between thirteen and fifteen sought the advice of a family planning clinic and asked for contraception – three times the figure of eight years ago. This is not the full picture of under-age sex, because we know that many buy condoms from chemists and slot machines, or may use no contraception at all. It was further revealed that the rate of teenage pregnancies is rising and more than 4,000 under-age girls a year opt for abortion.

Social commentator William Oddie considers it 'deplorable that clinics give contraceptives to these girls without telling their parents. Parents need to know that their children are having sex at an age when they're too young emotionally but also physically.' [3]

So when does childhood end and adulthood begin? It was only in the 1960s that the 'teenager' was first recognised – a fertile, untapped socio-economic group with money, ready and waiting for the growing advertising monster to target and attack. It seems that entry into adulthood gets younger every year and the real loss a nation should mourn is the loss of the innocence of childhood. The shocking truth is that by the time many are thirteen, they have experienced sexual activities far too intense for their tender years to understand, and consider 'innocence' and 'purity' a quality far too humiliating to treasure.

> **The shocking truth is that by the time many are thirteen, they have experienced sexual activities far too intense for their tender years to understand, and consider 'innocence' and 'purity' a quality far too humiliating to treasure.**

child mothers

> blame society, not these tragic children
> – angela lambert [4]

Pregnancies among girls under the age of sixteen rose by 11 per cent during the year 1996. Almost one in every 100 girls of fifteen or under fell pregnant before reaching the legal age for sex. More than half had abortions, around 4,550. The rate is now higher than in the early seventies when the Sexual Revolution among teenagers led to the Pill being prescribed for under sixteens.

Are these statistics a reflection of the sex-obsessed age in which we live where sexual adventure is considered a normal and natural part of growing up? Many would wholeheartedly agree that society is reaping the bitter fruit of a relaxation of moral standards and that we are now faced with the enormity of the consequences.

Others believe this trend is due to the easy availability of contraception. A major high street store has initiated a policy of providing free contraception to the young. Hugh McKinney, Chairman of the Conservative Family Campaign, says, 'The blame is squarely on the contraception and sex education industry for encouraging teenagers to regard under-age sex as a norm. The way to stop under-age girls getting pregnant is to encourage them to stop having sex.' [5] Family and Youth Concern believe 'most parents will be appalled to find that a major high street store is adopting a policy which could be so damaging'. [6] Victoria Gillick added her weight to the protest by saying that this 'will do nothing to help vulnerable children'. [6]

The high street store in question contested these remarks, saying they are providing a valuable service, in liaison with health experts, by supplying advice and education as well as contraception.

Many are calling for a ban on clinics providing contraception to girls under sixteen. This could be interpreted as a condemnation of sex education but they are separate issues. Despite the fact that opinion will always be divided over this issue, the root of the situation needs to be attended to and not merely the symptoms. It is all too easy to blame these under-age players for their actions – maybe we should look elsewhere. Maybe we should look in the direction of the explicit and degrading nature of today's films and videos or the satellite and cable programmes which are being produced; or maybe we should create an uproar about the promiscuous content of many of the teenage magazines or song lyrics; or maybe we should be more than a little concerned about the child-models who are appearing on the fashion catwalks.

The emerging generation often reflects the values they see lived out and promoted by their elders, so if we don't like what we see, who is to blame?

> we've removed the taboos which provided a safety
> net and replaced them with laissez-faire
> permissiveness and created a world where sex has
> become a children's game – *daily mail* **commentator** [7]

... society is reaping the bitter fruit of a relaxation of
moral standards and ... we are now faced with the
enormity of the consequences.

i do ... i don't

> teenage girls are less likely than boys to want a
> traditional marriage and family. more women are
> choosing to follow careers and the survey underlines
> the trend among young women to look to make
> their lives alone without the aid of men
> **– pearl assurance survey 1998** [8]

We are living in a post-marriage culture where it is far more
fashionable to 'live together' than seal a bond of love and
partnership in the form of a marriage vow. The 1996 figures from
the Office for National Statistics revealed the continuing decline
of the traditional family, with the proportion of babies across
England and Wales born outside of marriage approaching four in
ten. Of 642,000 births in 1996, 37 per cent were out of wedlock –
14 per cent higher than ten years ago. [9]

Nearly six out of ten of those born outside marriage were
registered by both parents giving the same address, whereas just
over 50,000 were registered by the mother alone. Critics point out
that living together provides a far less stable environment for
children than marriage, with a cohabitation on average lasting

only two and a half years, compared to more than nine for the average marriage. Figures for 1996 show that the number of weddings was the lowest since the First World War.

People have opted to 'live together' rather than marry for a variety of reasons. One of the main reasons for this decision is a lack of belief in marriage, perhaps due to witnessing their parents' divorce; or as a reaction to the divorce statistics with more than a third of marriages ending in divorce; or due to the desire to have many relationships rather than commit to one. Perhaps, surrounded by unfaithfulness, broken promises and infidelity, people have decided in this disposable age that permanency is a difficult thing to anticipate and therefore see no point in exchanging vows promising 'till death do us part'.

Co-habiting before marriage doesn't guarantee wedded bliss, however. A study by Dr David Pepenoe of Rutgers University New Jersey, has revealed that those who co-habit are 48 per cent more likely to divorce than couples who don't. The old adage may be true – it is marriage that keeps the love alive and not love that keeps the marriage alive. Dr Pepenoe also discovered that living together increases the risk of domestic violence.

Others want to check out their sexual compatibility before they think about marriage. Sex, however, is only part of the relation-ship and should not stand alone as a deciding factor for marriage. Long term covenant is also about friendship, respect, love, commitment, faithfulness, maturing together, and the physical act of sexual intimacy cannot be separated from all of these. Sex is not only physical, but emotional and spiritual, and advocates of marriage affirm that the best place for sexual intercourse is within a marriage covenant. It is not about a 'piece of paper' but about what this paper symbol represents.

> sex has become one of the most discussed subjects
> of modern times. the victorians pretended it did not
> exist; the moderns pretend that nothing else exists
> **– fulton j. sheen**

same sex

> they are the new village people. scores of housing
> developments specially adapted for homosexual
> residents are being built across britain as companies
> take advantage of the growing strength of the 'pink
> pound'. housing gay people has become lucrative
> **– *sunday times*** [10]

One of the biggest areas of change over the last three decades relates to the rights of gays and lesbians and the growing acceptance of their relationships as being normal rather than unnatural.

Sexual attraction to and preference for the same sex has historically been treated as perverse – creating a barrage of descriptives such as 'queer', and classifying the social fear or aversion to them as homophobia. Gay people have also endured extreme discrimination in every way and have often been ostracised from the rest of society in such a way that they have retreated to ghettos or suffered in silence.

In the nineteenth century, the German neuro-psychologist Richard von Krafft-Ebing considered homosexuality to be a disease, a hereditary neuropathic disorder, aggravated by excessive masturbation. Sigmund Freud joined the debate by adding that it could result from childhood experiences, particularly the lack of a parent of the same sex with whom to identify. Despite the opposition, and after many other studies, by 1974 homosexuality was removed from the list of mental disorders by the American Psychiatric Association.

In the 1940s Dr A. C. Kinsey conducted a famous investigation into human sexuality and identified everyone as falling somewhere on a continuum from 0, an exclusively homosexual bias, to 6, an exclusively heterosexual bias. Between those poles, people are found with dual, indeterminate or fluctuating sexual orientation. He concluded that 4 per cent of white American men are exclusively homosexual throughout their lives, and 10 per cent for up to three years. His findings have often been distorted by others and his sampling methods criticised.

Homosexuality in Britain was decriminalised in 1967 with homosexual activities legal for partners over the age of eighteen only in private. The Sexual Offences Act eleven years earlier declared sexual activity involving a young man or woman under the age of sixteen to be a criminal offence. Interestingly the law does not specifically set an age of consent for sexual activity between two women, but it is generally considered to be the same as for two men.

> gay issues have hit the mainstream but that doesn't make for a quiet political life – carla power [11]

There has been considerable pressure to treat homosexual couples in the same way as heterosexual couples and lower the age of consent to sixteen. The House of Commons, in a free vote of conscience, approved this move but the House of Lords voted in July 1998 not to make gay sex legal at sixteen. Another free vote in the Commons has once again supported the lowering of the age of consent, opting for equality for all. At the time of writing, there is still considerable opposition from the House of Lords and whether they will give final approval is still questionable. Many feel that Britain is out of step with other countries, as in Northern Ireland *all* sex is legal at seventeen; and in other European countries the age of consent is as low as fourteen in Pisa and Florence in Italy, fifteen in France and sixteen in Germany, although Gunter Dworek of the Gay Men's Association in Germany remarks, 'We're no longer criminalised but the law doesn't recognise us in any other way.' Italy's gay political movement has been a quiet affair due to the Church's role in public life and gay activist Franco Grillini jokes, 'There's only one person to whom you can admit you're gay – the priest at confession!' [11]

nurture or nature?

A considerable amount of analysis has been put into understanding homosexuality and lesbianism. Could it be the result of a gay gene? There is no conclusive evidence that a person is born homosexual or heterosexual even though chromosomal factors may produce feminine characteristics in men and masculine characteristics in women. Lewis Wolberg's essay on homosexuality explains, 'Chromosome counts and endocrine studies in homosexuals show no more than the average number of deviations. Male or female anatomical sex characteristics are established at the time of conception; but environmental factors influence the individual's later acceptance of gender role.' [12]

Advocates of the environmental theory place causal factors at the feet of an overbearing and possessive mother or a weak father. Other determinants are thought to be a bad experience in childhood, or a lack of intimate bonding, flesh to flesh, with one of the parents. Everyone's sexual development is unique and a child's sense of identity develops from the relationship with the parent figure of the same sex. Disturbances in parent-child relationships, a perceived rejection by a child's same-sex parent and a deficit in affirmation, affects the individual's security and in adulthood the emotional need for love and acceptance may become a sexual need.

Whether one's sexual orientation is decided by nurture or nature, the issue is incredibly delicate and complex. Whatever the contributing factors, many regard the resulting sexual activity as a matter of personal choice.

normalisation

> it's 28 years since several hundred lesbians and gay
> men had the initiative to protest on the streets of
> london for their recognition, equality and 'gay
> pride'. such courage and determination has evolved
> into britain's largest annual park festival, where
> celebrities are eager to appear and the masses flock
> to watch them – *everywoman* [13]

The process of normalising homosexuality and lesbianism has taken great strides in the last two decades. We are living in times when codes support positive discrimination in favour of homosexuals and lesbians, from the ability to obtain a housing mortgage without too much antagonistic questioning, to local councils asking gay and lesbian couples to adopt children due to difficulties in recruiting suitable couples. Although this has caused severe opposition, with reactionary remarks such as 'This is a shocking example of a liberal dogma gone mad, gays and lesbians as a family unit are completely unnatural'[14] from the chairman of the Merseyside Community Standards Association, the process is going ahead and will presumably be a model for other authorities to follow.

106

More and more media space is being given over to gay issues and celebrities. Dyke TV and Channel 4's Gay Night among countless other examples, celebrate sexual diversity and personalise gay people within art, music, film and television. It is increasingly fashionable to 'come out' although each 'outing' has a story to tell. Ellen de Generes decided to 'come out' in the public setting of her sitcom *Ellen*, which did not sit too comfortably with the powers that be, and eventually her show was axed. Although George Michael's orientation was known within the private world, his act of lewd behaviour in a toilet in Beverley Hills confirmed what the public at large had previously only speculated over. However, his 'coming out' did not seem to affect record sales negatively – in fact quite the opposite. His album *The Best of George Michael* went to number one in the charts and his opening words on the televised interview with Michael Parkinson were 'I didn't realise that to get on this show, I had to get my willy out.'

The process of normalising homosexuality and lesbianism has taken great strides in the last two decades.

coming out

A long line of public figures have been courageous and honest enough to disclose their sexual orientation. Some have done so cautiously whereas others have shouted from the rooftops. However, some have either been 'outed' by others or have been caught in 'a predicament' which has demanded an explanation. Singer kd lang came out in a blaze of glory, something she possibly regretted later, posing for a *Vanity Fair* cover in a barbershop clinch with Cindy Crawford. Madonna was impressed: 'Elvis is alive and she's beautiful.' There had already been huge speculation about her sexuality but this almost 'tongue-in-cheek' photoshoot unequivocally claimed the territory for lang.

Some politicians have also voluntarily 'come out' whilst others have been subjected to involuntary exposure. This propensity to declare sexual orientation will continue due to the growing conviction that heterosexuality is not the only acceptable way to live. In fact, some are treated as heroes. One thing that will remain is a preoccupation with how others choose to live, not simply those in the public eye who adorn the pages of *Hello* magazine, but 'ordinary folk' who make up most of humanity. People are interesting and that will never change. Perhaps the nature of an individual's sexuality may become less important in the future and what will really matter is whether or not you are monogamous and faithful!

The Internet is a treasure trove for those seeking articles on gay rights, chat sessions and hard-core gay pornography. Lesbians can even order a baby on the Net. Two ladies found a donor father from a web site and paid £280 for a man's frozen sperm to be delivered. The web site belongs to a company called 'NewLife' which says 'it helps people who haven't had the chance to bring a child into the world'.[15] They can choose the height, weight, age, nationality, income level and personality of the child's biological father, even select his sexual orientation and educational background.

Some lesbian partners approach gay or 'understanding' friends to donate sperm and cases have been known where a gay male donates sperm to a lesbian couple because it not only fulfils their dream of having a baby, it also fulfils his yearning to be a father. In a particular case, documented by a television company, the donor father visited the couple daily and the child is growing up with two mothers in the home and a father who lives close by.

There are obviously health dangers from ordering frozen sperm over the Internet. The risk of contracting HIV is ever present.

Those buying sperm in this way have no guarantee that it has been screened effectively for disease. Yvonne Stayti, of the campaign group Concern for Family and Womanhood, says, 'What these women are doing is against the natural order of things. It is completely horrendous. If these women want a child so badly then nature says they should get married and bring the child up in a stable and secure relationship. Just because more lesbians are opting for motherhood, doesn't make it right.' [15]

Right or wrong, situations like the above are happening at great speed with the assistance of medical and genetic breakthrough. What was once inconceivable is now possible, and what is now possible is unbelievable. This brave new world we have entered seems to be more advanced in technology than in the ability to evaluate how these breakthroughs will affect morality and culture.

Perhaps the nature of an individual's sexuality may become less important in the future and what will really matter is whether or not you are monogamous and faithful!

the new family

there can be few more graphic indicators of the traditional family's decline in modern britain than the new format for the revived game show, 'ask the family'. all types of entrants will be welcome, including single parents, uncles, step-fathers and same-sex partners – **leo mckinstry** [16]

Society has changed considerably since the programme *Ask The Family* began in 1968. There are new patterns of domestic life which reflect the normalisation of a variety of behaviours and lifestyles.

Critic Leo McKinstry remarks, 'Ethics have disappeared completely, and soaps such as *Casualty* and *EastEnders* continually promote homosexuality while presenting family life as nothing more than a source of conflict, brutality and repression.' [16]

On entering the new century, it is doubtful that the 'traditional family' will return to its original format. Some believe the nuclear family to be too exclusive anyway and welcome the idea of extended family, i.e. embracing single people and non-blood relationships, into the fold.

In primary school education, children as young as five are taught to be positive about being gay, and not to be discriminatory about other creeds and choices. In politics, Culture Secretary Chris Smith explained, 'It is time to recognise that families come in all shapes and sizes, and what matters is the validity of the family unit rather than how it is constructed.' [16]

Rather than harping on about how it used to be, surely it is more beneficial to hope that values such as trust, friendship, loyalty and respect will be demonstrated within these new models of family.

unholy orders

> if you can bless budgerigars and battleships, you can bless two people who love each other
> – malcolm johnson, pastoral care adviser [17]

Within the Christian Church, there are radical clergy who accept referrals for blessing single-sex unions. This disclosure has threatened a new split within the Church between those who are labelled as 'liberals' and those who are 'traditionalists'. The traditionalists believe that homosexual practice and single-sex unions are not compatible with teaching from the Bible.

110

The Lesbian and Gay Christian Movement claims that there are churches in the UK where priests carry out gay blessings and it has been estimated that in 1998 over five hundred gay unions were blessed, despite a ban on this unorthodox ceremony. The debate over homosexuality and the Church will not go away, in fact it is escalating.

Alan Smithson, Bishop of Jarrow, believes, 'The church ought to strengthen and support any loving relationship which is permanent, exclusive and faithful. It should find a way to sanction this covenant.'[17] This public display of defiance was supported by Malcolm Johnson, the Bishop of London's pastoral care adviser, who believes 'gay and lesbian love to be godly and good'. [17]

Although many supporters of same-sex unions within the Church hoped to see an acceptance of homosexuality within the Church of England, a huge majority of bishops are still maintaining that homosexual behaviour is incompatible with the Bible, gay weddings should be outlawed and homosexuals should not be ordained as priests. Although decisions taken by the Lambeth Conference of Anglican Leaders Worldwide are not legally binding, they do assert a powerful influence of opinion.

Opinion is divided, hotly debated and wholeheartedly sustained on both sides of the argument. An official split seems inevitable with the prospect of already existing gay fellowships commanding much higher profile and focus, and many more will no doubt be established. A church in America is planning to build a vast cathedral in Dallas to seat up to 2,500 worshippers. The existing building belonging to the 'Cathedral of Hope' seats 900 and most services are so oversubscribed that three have to be held each Sunday. They are part of the Universal Fellowship of Metropolitan Community Churches, and is the largest gay church in the world with parishes in London, Manchester, Newcastle, Birmingham and Exeter. [18]

> love the sinner but hate the sin. for what shall it
> profit a church, if it gain a liberal worldview, and
> lose its own soul – **comment, *daily mail***

An official split seems inevitable with the prospect of
already existing gay fellowships commanding much
higher profile and focus, and many more will no doubt
be established.

homophobia

> the category of 'homosexual' is a late-nineteenth
> century invention. the current model to work from is
> of a continuum – in this sense few can be described
> as simply homosexual or heterosexual, but that we
> are looking at a scale of dispositional capacities for
> sexual arousal. given we are sexual beings, are
> there any relationships that are non-sexual? –
> **martin scott, *the bible and homosexuality*** [19]

Homophobia has been widespread and noticeably apparent within
the Church. Historically, far more emphasis has been given to
homosexual practice than to other forms of moral failure
mentioned in the Bible such as greed, pride and envy. Until the
post-war period in the long history of the Church there were few,
if any, dissenting voices to the view that Scripture and nature teach
that homosexual behaviour is, without exception, wrong.

Careful and considered analysis has recently been taking place,
even though in most cases the conclusions are the same. Although
Martin Scott in his booklet, *The Bible and Homosexuality*,

summarises his research by saying that homosexual activity is condemned in both testaments, and states that heterosexual intercourse is endorsed within marriage with the only other option being celibacy, he does have some illuminating additions. He broadens out the subject to the bigger issue of sexuality and suggests, 'we cannot assume that a person who is heterosexual in orientation needs no healing in their sexuality, for all sexuality is fallen. One's orientation can be seen as one part of one's sexuality, and further one's sexuality is but one aspect of what it means to be a person. The goal for all people is to be healed.' [19]

Scott continues by saying, 'far from denying those of homosexual orientation same-sex affection, there is a great need for that expression – indeed not just for those of a particular orientation. The church must lead the way in modelling relation-ships.' He calls for a more 'non-judgemental approach towards those outside the community of faith, while loving discipline is exercised toward those inside. At some stage, it might well be right and necessary for the church to make an apology to the gay community for the persecution that has come to it, but in doing so I am not suggesting that truth is compromised.' [19]

Brave words indeed, and some will find this approach difficult to swallow. It seems an essential position to adopt in this age where reconciliation is of such great importance. Wise are the generations who strive for reconciliation whilst accepting diversity.

> the christian community must respond to the issue of homosexuality and to homophile people in a way that combines love and truth, compassion and biblical integrity. the debate among christians about homosexuality is, implicitly, a debate about how to do theology – **christopher townsend**

faithless or faithful?

Hardly a week goes by without the media reporting evidence of broken relationships, or marriage separations, or divorce, or crimes of passion, or adulterous affairs, or one-night stands – all leading to a culture of promiscuity. People admit that it is hard to stay faithful to a partner and contend that it is unnatural to be monogamous; others confess to seeing little wrong with 'sleeping around' or having an unemotional but sexual liaison whilst on holiday or on business, even though they may be married or in a relationship.

We are all on a search for love – there is a deep-seated desire to give love and receive love. There is also the need to belong and to be accepted and valued. These needs being so central to humanity, have the potential to invigorate and satisfy or to be painful and cause immense personal scars. In searching for love people can search for pleasure instead and can leave a lot of broken relationships along the way. In hoping to be satisfied, people can develop an insatiable desire for sexual thrill without commitment.

There is an appalling lack of role-model relationships which promote and manage to outwork faithfulness. Especially within films and television, adultery and infidelity are the norm and, as a viewer, we can get carried along by the plot and feel pleased when lovers meet, and the husband is rejected. (Even if this goes against a deep-seated belief in staying faithful.)

The final trilogy of *Men Behaving Badly*, which was watched by millions, treated Gary and Tony's unfaithfulness as inevitable and almost irrelevant. Amidst the comedy of the characters, there is something tragic about this decay of trust and loyalty. More positive displays of faithfulness and fidelity are required, but will it get good ratings?

> often the seeds of adultery have been sown long
> before the fruit is harvested. factors which lead
> people into an affair are often little to do with sex
> itself: unresolved conflict, a desire to 'get back at' a
> spouse, loneliness, absence from the home,
> infatuation, low self-esteem or just plain boredom
> – **elaine storkey,** *the search for intimacy* [20]

**There is an appalling lack of role-model relationships
that promote and manage to outwork faithfulness.**

crisis point

> how can a young person choose when the
> advertising campaigns use sex to sell a product,
> when magazines encourage exploitation and when
> friends are fascinated for juicy information?
> – **aids care, education and training (acet)** [21]

There are many sexual diseases, syphilis, chancroid, herpes, genital
warts … In fact an epidemic of syphilis has been traced as far back
as 1494, and some would even suggest that sexual illness was
identified in biblical times. Remaining a serious threat to public
health, it was a major cause of death until penicillin was discovered
by Sir Alexander Fleming in 1929 and used effectively in fighting
infection in 1941.

> there is nothing new about people being ill as a
> result of sex. you may feel that the best way to
> avoid sexual diseases is to reduce the number of
> partners. life is not that simple. one partner infects
> another; and after a year, perhaps both have new
> partners, and infect one other person each
> **– dr patrick dixon, *the rising price of love*** [22]

Regardless of medical breakthroughs, there are at least 250 million new cases of sexually transmitted diseases each year throughout the world, according to the World Health Organisation figures of 1990. Figures released by Aids Care, Education and Training (ACET), on World Aids Day 1998 stated that in the UK, one in ten people under the age of twenty-five may be carrying a sexually transmitted infection. People are encouraged to seek medical diagnosis and attention if they develop any STD symptoms or are concerned.

aids [23]

> the level of acceptance of homosexuality reached by
> the late 1970's was countered in the early 80's by
> the spread of 'acquired immune deficiency
> syndrome' or aids, by which the male homosexual
> population is especially hard-hit. this led to
> increasing fear and social ostracism of homosexuals
> **– lewis wolberg** [12]

A major crisis affecting behaviour and attitudes has been the global onset of AIDS. Within the last ten years, significant steps have been made regarding the understanding of the HIV virus and the risks of infection. Aggressive prevention campaigns,

116

educational strategies and statistical information have attempted to replace fear and ignorance with reality, practical help and advice. In this country, the homosexual community was first affected and consequently AIDS was labelled the 'gay disease'. This belief was soon challenged when evidence revealed that the HIV virus did not belong to this one community alone, but transcended all boundaries of colour, race and sexual orientation.

The risk of HIV infection was now considered possible through heterosexual activity, through drug use as well as through homosexual activity. In the early stages, projected figures of HIV infection abounded, threatening an explosion beyond belief and creating a climate of immense fear and paranoia, only made more intense by ignorance.

> a whole new generation is sick of hearing of the dangers of AIDS and think they are exaggerated. many feel it is a false alarm and others say 'what the hell, you only live once' – **dr john money, 1992**

Dr Michael Merson, director of the World Health Organisation's global programme on AIDS, remarked, 'Aggressive prevention campaigns can make a real difference in the ultimate size of the pandemic. If we seize this opportunity, millions of people may be spared infection by the year 2000.' Current figures estimate that over 30 million people worldwide are now living with HIV and AIDS and at least a third of these are young people aged ten to twenty-four. In this particular age group 7,000 are infected with HIV out of a total of 16,000 new cases per day around the world. It is reported to be spreading faster than previously thought and worst-case estimates of ten years ago are set to be realised. By the year 2000, between 40 and 60 million people will be HIV-positive. Worldwide, HIV is transmitted mainly by heterosexual sex.

In the UK over 15,000 have developed AIDS, of whom 72 per cent have died. Another 16,000 are HIV-positive. Whilst the number of new AIDS cases is apparently falling, the rate of new HIV infections remains steady. This means that people are living with the virus and requiring expensive treatment. [21]

number fatigue

When faced with statistics, it is easy to become numb and forget that each digit represents a person. And unless reality bites close to home, many remain unaffected by the tragic loss of life. However, films such as *Philadelphia*, with Tom Hanks playing a lawyer who gets fired from his firm because he has AIDS, and the history of the epidemic in *And the Band Played On*, have all helped to personalise the figures. Personal testimony contains a depth and reality that prompts thought and reflection, and hopefully responsible action. All this is needed, along with innovative programmes of education and training to combat the crisis.

> especially in the gay community, people have been left with such a crater around them, they're just in despair – **composer alan menken who lost his collaborator, lyricist howard ashman** [24]

Hope and medicine are still calling for a cure. New drugs have been developed to control symptoms but Dr Patrick Dixon in his book, *The Genetic Revolution*, is uncertain about when a cure will be found. 'By the turn of the century we should have seen some major advances towards developing effective treatments, although safety testing and high costs are likely to delay widespread use and a permanent cure is likely to be much further away.' [25]

When faced with statistics, it is easy to become numb and forget that each digit represents a person.

winds of change

A crisis causes people to evaluate and re-examine established beliefs or modes of behaviour. The AIDS crisis has been no different. It has prompted young people, in particular, to assess their own sexual behaviour and re-examine their values. Motivation to adopt safer sex has resulted in a condom culture as well as a growing trend towards fewer sexual partners, monogamy and even sexual abstinence.

The emergence of a generation realising that the consequences of the 1960s' search for sexual utopia have been destructive as well as liberating, is signalling some interesting new trends. Positive alternatives are being offered. Celibacy or sexual abstinence is becoming a considered choice, free from the stigma of inferiority and oddness that it has attracted over past decades. The positive alternative of monogamy or fewer sexual partners is also being advocated, helping to combat the sexually transmitted disease crisis as well as promoting the advantages of 'commitment for life'. The tragic divorce rate, the trauma of family breakdown, the surge in teenage pregnancies, the availability and trauma of abortion have all resulted in a re-assessment of values. How *much* this re-assessment will affect actual behaviour remains to be seen.

There is a heartcry from all those who are hurt, confused and disillusioned. Joining the sound of discontent are the many multitudes of people for whom the promise of freedom was precisely what life was all about. The smell of freedom has been bitter to taste and there is a new radicalism that could potentially be the antidote for the poison that has infected society.

many have experienced parental break-up and
divorce, but they retain a traditional belief in family
and authority that harks back to the 1950's
– **survey results, *independent*, nov 1998** [26]

The smell of freedom has been bitter to taste and there
is a new radicalism that could potentially be the antidote for the poison that has infected society.

true love waits

some things are worth waiting for ... especially sex
– **john bicknell** [27]

Inspired by an American organisation, the Berkhamsted based
'True Love Waits' is on a mission to 'champion the lost art of
virginity'.

John Bicknell, known as the arch-enemy of pre-marital sex,
claims to have 10,000 card carrying virgins in his True Love Waits
movement, which is based on Christian principles. As well as
writing and promoting his book, *Sexy But ... True Love Waits*,
Bicknell wishes to 'take the message into schools to discourage
young people from sexual intercourse until they are ready for its
consequences', writes Melanie McFadyean. [27]

Critics, such as Alison Hadley of the Brook Advisory Service,
believe that this 'just say no' approach gives teenagers a 'negative
view which distorts the reality that sex before marriage is widely
accepted'. Others are critical of the TLW message, referring to it as
a scare tactic, maintaining that teenagers act more responsibly
when sex is regarded liberally and openly.

However, the TLW message is more than just an encouragement to say '*no*', it explains why keeping your virginity until marriage is the best option. An eighteen year old called Laura told McFadyean, 'I don't want to pollute myself. If I had sex, I would lose my purity, I'd feel I'd let myself down and God down.' [27]

red hot and holy

From every corner of society, people are longing for a 'moral revival'. Clever anecdotes which superficially gloss over the moral bankruptcy of hedonism are not enough. It goes deeper than that. New role models are needed to promote an alternative framework upon which life values can then be formulated. These voices either need to be pitched in the places of influence for today's culture: in music, in magazines, in the fashion houses and out of the mouths of popular-prophets, or from a moral grassroots movement, the like of which we have never experienced before in the history of humankind.

From every corner of society, people are longing for a 'moral revival'. Clever anecdotes that superficially gloss over the moral bankruptcy of hedonism are not enough.

♂ Gendertalk

are men an endangered species? [1]

> losing out to women in the workplace, confused
> about their role in an increasingly feminised society,
> and marginalised as fathers, modern males see
> themselves as creatures to be pitied
> – leo mckinstry [2]

A hundred species a day – four species an hour – are apparently being pushed into evolutionary oblivion, and campaigns to save the Indian tiger or the Caribbean manatee are accumulating global support. There could, however, be another species of mammal on the endangered list!

It is the category of the human male which appears to be 'in crisis', as all around his natural habitat is changing. For many years now, he has been reeling from the domestic turmoil caused by the unchaining of women from the kitchen sink. The rethinking and repositioning of gender roles within the home have destabilised a once secure and familiar environment.

If that was not enough, recent medical and scientific advances are excluding him from the baby process; and to top it all he even faces sexual redundancy with the release of the tabloid-titled 'Thrill Pill', providing female orgasm in tablet form. A final and agonising death blow is being dealt to the traditional male role of hunter and provider. Peter Downes, in his book *Can Boys Do Better?*, comments, 'The changing world of work seems to be undermining boys' confidence and self esteem with traditional manual jobs being replaced by more technology and consumer-based professions requiring feminine skills.'

It would appear that in this fast technological age, the archaic definitions of what constitutes masculine and feminine have become claustrophobic. Inherited words of wisdom such as 'big boys don't cry' and 'a woman's place is in the home' have become counter productive. Behaviour according to certain prescribed gender patterns has possibly stunted growth on an individual and societal level, creating the endemic gender confusion in evidence today.

According to Downes, in view of the threat to the male of the species, it is time for 'society to redefine masculinity … and feminise the male to give him a new role in the future world'. This modern-day search to redefine masculinity and femininity contains many snares. We must guard against simply replacing one type of restrictive definitions with another set, albeit different, but equally as limiting. This will surely yield problems further down the line. Both sexes do have a lot of old behavioural clothes to throw away – but let's not be too quick to put on new ones!

To understand the present, we need to look into the past. The journey of the two sexes has been a complex one.

It is the category of the human male which appears to be 'in crisis', as all around his natural habitat is changing.

a long and winding road

> when your husband returns from work:
>
> prepare yourself. take 15 minutes to rest so you'll be refreshed when he arrives. touch up your make-up, put a ribbon in your hair. he has just been with a lot of work-weary people.
>
> arrange his pillow and offer to take off his shoes. speak in a low, soothing and pleasant voice.
>
> over the cooler months of the year you should prepare and light a fire for him to unwind by. your husband will feel he has reached a haven of rest and order, and it will give you a lift too. after all, catering for his comfort will provide you with immense personal satisfaction.
>
> make the evening his, never complain if he comes home late or goes out to dinner, or other places of entertainment without you.
>
> don't ask questions about his actions or question his judgement or integrity. remember he is the master of the house and as such will always exercise his will with fairness and truthfulness. you have no right to question him.
>
> **– extract from a 1960s home economics book**

One of the most important developments in the history of humankind has been the progress of women's rights. Many throughout the years have faithfully and unswervingly addressed the realities of universal inequality and oppression because of a fundamental belief that all human beings are equal. The Feminist Movement, believing that women are different from men but have a legitimate and equal claim to social and economic rights, has sought to expose injustice, provoke change and generate an essential shift in mindset. Equality not sameness.

There has been a significant amount of 'feminism-fobia', not just from men but also from women. Many shy away from the f-word because of the way the media, in particular, has portrayed and misrepresented it. Certain stereotypes have been associated with the word, and even though people believe in the essence of what feminism represents, they cannot sit comfortably with the image which has been attached to it. It has almost become a dirty word, and although women want equal pay, access to better jobs and an environment free from discrimination, they will not admit to being feminist. Images of rebellion, lesbianism, and a desire to be disassociated from the male oppressors are so often attached to the word. Those images from the radical end of feminism are so strong, they stick.

Liberal feminism, the group to which the majority belong, is primarily concerned with changing society to help women gain greater personal freedom, pursuing equal rights, legal reforms and non-sexist education.

Equality not sameness.

the first wave

> never doubt that a small group of thoughtful committed citizens can change the world. indeed, it is the only thing that ever has – **margaret mead**

Women played a major role in the 1789 French Revolution, causing some women to argue that if they had the task of bringing up the new citizens, then they should also have status. In Olympe de Gourges' pamphlet *Rights of a Woman*, she wrote, 'Woman is born free and her rights are the same as those of man ... if women have the right to go to the scaffold, they must also have the right to go to Parliament.' Parisian women formed political clubs but these were soon outlawed by the male leaders, re-affirming that a woman's place is in the home.

The women of Britain were watching the events in France with great interest, and this generated some reactionary writing. At the same time, eighteenth-century Enlightenment thinking 'gave the whole world a new look,' says Elaine Storkey in *What's Right with Feminism*. Storkey continues, 'Society was reappraised, there was a focus on autonomous man, man on his own, man come of age. Along with renewed interest in the rights of man came an awakening to the rights of women. If they were part of the common rationality of humanity, what was the reason for one sex to be denied the privileges, status, education and legal rights of the other sex?' [3]

Mary Wollstonecraft, a journalist and translator, produced *A Vindication of the Rights of Women* as a response to a publication entitled *The Rights of Man*. Wollstonecraft's book favouring women's liberation was widely read, but she was dismissed by the male conservative press.

Meanwhile in America, in the late eighteenth century, women made up a large part of the black and white revival congregations. Although women were not supposed to preach, some ignored this. Black women realised it was not enough to be free from the slavery of whites, they needed also to be free from the domination of men. Black feminist Sojourner Truth was particularly outspoken, arguing that women should have the vote.

> the most flagrant and influential anti-slavery novel
> was written by a christian and a woman
> – **elaine storkey** [4]

Along with a growing social conscience in late eighteenth/early nineteenth-century Britain, there was also a growing awareness of God and the dignity of both men and women. An evangelical journal in 1860, edited and controlled by women, challenged the foundational idea that women's satisfaction only came through marriage. This early Christian feminism had a positive bias towards the weak and oppressed. The temperance societies, which were concerned with the effects of alcohol on family life, often resulting in wife abuse, prostitution and economic hardship, contained many women within it who were Christian feminists. Many women were involved in the movement to abolish slavery, although towards the end it was the male campaigners who had the political power to bring it to an end.

> women's call for the vote was echoing around the
> world. it was first answered in aotearoa/new
> zealand in 1893 – *new internationalist* [5]

Millicent Garrett Fawcett, at the age of twenty-two, set out on her first speaking tour of Britain for women's suffrage, abolishing the arguments that were used against giving women the vote. It was said that women were intellectually inferior, physically inferior, too pure to be involved in politics and if they were given the vote, it would distract them from the family and home. Against all odds, women pressed on, believing that they did have rights to education and to hold power.

Emmeline Pankhurst and her two daughters, Sylvia and

Christabel, organised mass meetings in Britain and drew crowds of up to 500,000. The infamous chaining of themselves to parliament railings caused civil disturbances and, in 1908, the Pankhursts were imprisoned. They went on a hunger strike and were force fed. Finally in 1918, women over the age of thirty were allowed to vote in Britain.

The first wave of feminism secured the vote.

the second wave

> the first problem for all of us, men and women, is not to learn, but to unlearn – **gloria steinhem**

During the 1960s feminism received fresh impetus. The excitement of the sexual liberation for women broadened their horizons. With new understanding of female sexual arousal and the introduction of the birth-control pill, women were beginning to form an identity that was not controlled by, or determined by, men. *The Feminine Mystique* by Betty Friedan was a bestseller in 1963, and Germaine Greer's *The Female Eunuch* was enlightening. Women found their voice and campaigned on specific issues such as childcare, health, domestic violence, education, the lack of reproductive rights and equal pay for work of equal value.

Women found their voice and campaigned on specific issues such as childcare, health, domestic violence, education, the lack of reproductive rights and equal pay for work of equal value.

the third wave — new feminism

> equality would make an immense difference to
> everyone. inequality breeds inequality. once you've
> broken that cycle of inequality, it wouldn't
> necessarily make everything nice, but it could
> possibly lead to a better society — **natasha walter** [6]

Feminism is taking a different direction from the seventies and eighties. That period was good for taking ground on personal life issues, but now the emphasis seems to be once more upon the tough questions of poverty and inequality.

There have been great advances regarding women choosing to work and finding alternative arrangements for their children. We have women in government and women in business. There is a better division of duties within the home between the man and the woman. There have been significant changes in the social scene for women and there is now more control for women over reproductive rights. There are more women in positions of influence, in education, in the media and there are women being ordained into the clergy. There are women who dress the way they choose rather than for their man and there are countless women in mainstream music. However, there is still more which remains unaccomplished and unjust.

Since the bill was passed allowing women to be ordained within the Church of England, two thousand have been ordained nationally, comprising a sixth of the total number of clergy in Britain. However, there are no female priests appointed to any of the royal chapels, and leading women clergy suggest that they have been sidelined because of traditional beliefs. Jean Mayland, one of the first women to be ordained in 1994, considers it to be 'another example of women being treated as second class citizens who are expendable and not to be taken seriously'. [7]

> much attention has been given to men losing out to women in the workplace, but women continue to make up the vast majority of low-paid workers. the average gross weekly wage for a woman is £185, compared with £374 for a man. in retirement, women are more likely to live in poverty than men — **leo mckinstry** [2]

Natasha Walter, author of *The New Feminism*, explains,

concrete issues are coming back again. We thought we'd dealt with them, but we haven't, and now we want to deal with them for good. If you look at women's poor body image, it is still because women feel they have to please men. You go into a working environment and the boss is more likely to be a man. That inequality encourages women to believe we're there on sufferance and if he gets bored with the way we look, we're out. That we have to be young, thin and cute or somehow we're vulnerable. If women had economic equality and power in the workplace, they'd be happy about throwing their weight around, literally as well as metaphorically. [8]

> the 'fit' woman, financially independent twenty and thirtysomething, doesn't rely on a man to pay her way, watches what she spends and plans for her financial future. men, far from feeling threatened, are increasingly seeking out such women as partners — **prudential insurance survey** [9]

There have been great advances … However, there is still more which remains unaccomplished and unjust.

what women want

In June 1995, the largest ever social audit of women's opinions in the UK began. The survey was co-ordinated by the Women's Communications Centre, and millions of green postcards asking the question, 'What do you want?', were distributed around the country by women's groups, trade unions, banks and shops, and were handed out outside supermarkets, inside public areas, or attached to magazines and regular mailings of organisations.

The answers were diverse: women have differing experiences and opinions, but some issues arose time and time again. They want: [10]

- more women in politics, industry and society, represented at the top and given greater opportunities
- a fair economy with an alleviation of poverty and its effect on women and children
- more women in media represented in top positions and less patronising offensive representations of them in newspapers and magazines
- a broader curriculum in education with an emphasis on communication and literacy
- better communication between the sexes and more co-operation with men
- respect in all areas of life and equality at work and equal pay

women want choices. not just for women but for men too. traditional 'male' and 'female' ways to behave in society are too restrictive. everyone should have the freedom to be who they want to be without fear of judgement by society
– what women want [10]

girl power

It's easy to look at the current climate and think that feminism has run its course and that we are now living in a post-feminist era. Thanks to the last one hundred and fifty years, women are considered a growth industry. In television, magazines and music in particular, we have seen a rise of women warriors who will not sit back and be dictated to by the historic male-dominated institutions. In typical pendulum style, the swing is in the excess position.

> the plug has been pulled on the boy bands of yesteryear. in the world of pop, sisters are now doing it for themselves – **alan jackson** [11]

Frank has heralded a new generation of magazines for women containing the underlying ethos that women have more interests than make-up and recipes. Added to the menu are politics, humanitarian issues and insights into contemporary culture, in the hope of 'giving women a voice'. I have been greatly amused by the choice of a male name for the title.

A front cover of *Music Week* declared, 'It's a girls' world'. In popular music there are now countless female stars riding high: Alanis Morissette, Sheryl Crow, Celine Dion, The Spice Girls, Nenah Cherry, All Saints, Bjork, Madonna. No doubt inspired by their forerunners who have blazed the trail for women in music: Aretha Franklin, Annie Lennox, Janis Joplin, Suzanne Vega and Chrissie Hynde. These women are not merely the archetypal 'backing singers' or the 'glam-on-stage' to please the men, but they are real artists, performers and songwriters in their own right. Female informed rock music has popularised feminism and brought it to the attention of mainstream culture.

There are women artists who champion the cause for equality, along with other issues of justice, through their music. They personify the feminist aims. Skin from Skunk Anansie, for example, does not conform to the stereotypical feminine look, and that is just her point. She leaps about on stage with unusual energy and her music is heavy. There are not many women playing that kind of music and she is a challenge to those who cannot see past the image to appreciate the music. Courteney Love is another example of a 'card carrying feminist' who expresses a rage within her music that reflects her life. She defies conformity.

> **These women are not merely the archetypal 'backing singers' or the 'glam-on-stage' to please the men. They are real artists, performers and songwriters in their own right.**

righteous babes [12]

Artists like Ani DiFranco represent a new breed of woman. Her songs are statements of womanhood and although she has not deliberately brought feminism into her music, she explains, 'my gender informs what I see and by nature my work is therefore feminist.'[12] She owns her own record company, as does Madonna and Queen Latifah, and runs 'Righteous Babes' in a principled, consistent way that reflects her political beliefs.

What is it about women and music which is selling more records than ever before and filling large venues? Girls with guitars, girls with pianos, girls with bands, girls with dancers: anything goes. Apparently 40 per cent of rock audiences are now women. The Lilith Fair tour, championed by Sarah McLaughlin, is a celebration of women in music and has been extremely successful around the world. Many are drawn to the rage and angst expressed in the self-penned songs of female artists. True stories of real life connect with women. Tori Amos expressed her own personal experience of rape in 'Me and a Gun', whereupon she convinced her record company to finance a national rape hotline in the US. Bearing in mind that US figures show that one in three women are raped and over a third of women are violently battered in marriage, this hotline was amazingly the first of its kind. Sinead O'Connor expresses her personal trauma of child abuse and she admits to being driven by this rage within her songwriting.

For so many years mainstream music has been male dominated, with songs reflecting male language and male perspectives. Female-informed music has tapped into an evident raving hunger for the world to be seen through the eyes of a woman. The industry has obviously noticed that feminism has bargaining power and targeted a whole new set of consumers. Previously to be feminist and in music meant that you had somehow to bury your sexuality but many artists have changed that, with Madonna being the prime example. She has flaunted her sexuality and remains a top selling artist with control over her career and also with her own record company.

> these days, putting out one's pretty power, one's sexual energy for popular consumption no longer makes you a bimbo, it makes you smart
> – elizabeth wurtzel, *bitch*, 1998

Female-informed music has tapped into an evident raving hunger for the world to be seen through the eyes of a woman.

the price of spice

Many women in music have criticised the Spice Girls for portraying feminism as glamour and image to teen and pre-teen audiences.

They remark that the Spice Girls are more about product sponsor-ship and manipulating the media with their half-clothed bodies, than about liberation and equality. The *girl power* slogan was no doubt a marketing tool dreamed up by the record company executives, and many feminists see this to be an empty slogan of female power, with the potential for profit only. DiFranco commented that this 'girl power' has 'sucked the life out of feminism and is nothing more than a meaningless bumper sticker'. [12]

The campaign for women's rights has come a long way. From being chained to parliament railings in the hope that one day women will get the vote, to filling huge concert venues for Lilith Fair. Feminism has persevered in speaking (or singing) out for social and economic equality. The Spice Girls are, however, a thorn in the side. How long do we have to put up with those humiliating and self-destructive words 'girl power' from the band that ate the world? They are role models for young girls who are enjoying the benefits of progress but are not appreciating the cost or the deeper issues involved. Their fans probably think that the history books of girl power have the Spice Girls on page one! If this man-made, highly marketable 'girl power' image continues, then I fear for the future of men and women.

Feminism is about equality, not power. It is *not* about adopting the very attitudes which feminists have derided in men and re-classifying them as virtues in women. It was never about replacing one form of power with another. It is about equality and partnership. Only if we stay close to the truth, that men and women are created equal and should have equal opportunity, will there be hope.

Feminism is about equality, not power. It is *not* about adopting the very attitudes which feminists have derided in men and re-classifying them as virtues in women.

the new ladette

A MORI poll has unveiled the women who copy men, behaving badly in public with loud, slobbish, pleasure seeking behaviour. Bel Mooney comments, 'What a victory. Equality is measured out in pints and piles of dirt, while the brainless, twittering, man-obsessed Ally McBeal and the tedious and limited *Bridget Jones's Diary* are both slavishly admired. Sad, sad, sad.' [13]

This 'ladette' attitude is getting Zoë Ball, Denise Van Outen and others noticed. Their behaviour is an obvious rebellion against the stereotypes which have existed for so long. So they join in and go even further, they are self-indulgent and it is a big bonus if they happen to be blonde and beautiful.

Documentaries on Sky TV of Brits abroad on holiday contain numerous ladettes who, by their flirtatious, anything-goes philosophy, achieve the real all time low of utterly debasing themselves on camera by trading their self-respect for a passing alcohol or drug-induced pleasure! However, they seem to have totally missed the point. By overtly expressing traits of independence and liberation from how women have been expected to behave, they enter the realm of the objectionable. Men should not behave like that, nor should women. I would have hoped we had more sense!

Fear not. Ladettes do grow up. Women like Ruby Wax and Bette Midler are possibly older examples of outrageous ladies who challenged the prevailing stereotypes. Listen to them now: they still have that spark of nonconformity but are much wiser. Millennial ladettes in training need new role models who tackle the important issues without compromising but stop short of humiliating themselves and the entire female race.

> **Millennial ladettes in training need new role models who tackle the important issues without compromising but stop short of humiliating themselves and the entire female race.**

the struggle

On a global level, women have been considered inferior. If this were not the case, there would be no struggle and no campaigning for equality. Statistics show that women produce half the world's food, yet constitute 70 per cent of the 1.3 billion absolute poor. They work two-thirds of the world's working hours, but own less than 1 per cent of the world's property. Of the world's one billion illiterates, two-thirds are women.

Women are victimised and abused. Between 85 and 114 million women and girls have undergone female genital mutilation, and a girl who doesn't undergo this rite of passage is considered, in certain cultures, to be unmarriageable. It is estimated that one-fourth of women worldwide are physically battered and in China, the one-child policy which began in 1979 caused a dramatic rise in infant girl deaths. These figures are the tip of the iceberg. [14]

The marriage service has been in question of late. The woman's promise to obey her husband, the 'natural' taking of his surname along with the symbolic act of being 'given away' by the father or stand-in, have been interpreted as indicating that the woman is the property of the man. According to Simon Andreae, 'The institution of marriage was often more about property and inheritance than individual commitment.'[15] Emphasis has often been on the bride being virginal and young, irrespective of how the man has behaved, and the white wedding dress and the veil are symbolic of the pure standards required by men of their brides. In some cultures, females who have, or are suspected to have had, sex before marriage can be executed with the approval of the community. Women also seek out medical assistance to restore broken hymens to give the appearance of being a virgin, and the custom of sheet showing reveals the deep-seated control that men have had over women.

There is also a demand for women to begin making speeches at wedding receptions, to end the practice of 'men only'. Changes have been made to the wedding ceremony, amending some of the wording with a view to making the vows equal and the vocabulary less sexist and more inclusive. This obviously has its critics among Anglican traditionalists, but is more in keeping with the progress which is happening in secular society.

woman

The history of how a woman has been perceived is complex and elaborate. There are many great books analysing the place of women within different cultures and centuries, which help us to appreciate the long and winding road that women have travelled. Of all the writings which emerged from the existentialist movement, Simone de Beauvoir's study of women, *The Second Sex*, was penetratingly incisive and a landmark in modern feminism.

She writes,

> By the time humankind reached the stage of written mythology and law, the patriarchate was definitely established: the males were to write the codes. It was natural for them to give women a subordinate position. Once sacred, she becomes impure. Eve, given to Adam to be his companion, worked the ruin of mankind. The pagan gods invent women and it is the first-born of these female creatures, Pandora, who lets loose all the ills of suffering humanity. Woman is thus dedicated to evil. 'There is a good principle, which has created order, light and man, and there is a bad principle, which has created chaos, darkness and woman,' said Pythagoras. The laws of Manu define woman as

a vile being who should be held in slavery. Leviticus likens her to the beasts of burden owned by the patriarch. The laws of Solon give her no rights. The Roman Code puts her under guardianship and asserts her 'imbecility'. Canon Law regards her as the 'devil's doorway'. The Koran treats women with utter scorn. [16]

Israeli rabbis would not teach women to read in case they looked upon Scripture and defiled it. St Jerome pronounced, 'Woman is a temple built over a sewer', and the general attitude in the early Christian world was that women were mistrustful and temptresses, bearing the whole blame for the sinfulness of the world.

What an inheritance!

> **women have been stereotyped as the sexual, the gullible, the errant, the weak, whilst men have been seen as the rational, the decisive, the strong component of humanity – elaine storkey, *contributions to christian feminism*** [17]

how feminine is your god?

> **until the emphasis on maleness in the image of god is redressed, the women of the world cannot be entirely liberated. if god is thought of as simply and exclusively male, then the very cosmos seems sexist – phil moore** [18]

Mary Daly suggests in her book, *Beyond God the Father*, that if 'God is male, then the male is God. The divine patriarch castrates women as long as he is allowed to live on in the human imagination.' [19]

The popular and traditional image of God is male. However, God is spirit and is neither male nor female. The Bible says, 'God created humankind in his image, in the image of God he created them; male and female.' [20] Gender is integral within humanity but not within God. God transcends male and female. The concept which has been used within Scripture is that of God being Father, which describes a relationship rather than a gender description. There are also references to the maternal aspects of God and some religious leaders, for example Mary Baker Eddy, have tried to emphasise these.

Consistently, God has been referred to using male terminology within a society where the male is the norm and the dominant culture. Some feminists are trying to redress the balance by calling God 'she'. However, this gives a picture which is just as biased as the scenario we have come from. The dominance of male imagery has caused women to feel alienated from the Christian faith and question whether they fit into a faith that worships a male God, contains a male Jesus and bestows the majority of leadership and power into the hands of men. Women have turned away from the Christian faith and sought spiritual solace elsewhere, in paganism for example or in goddess feminism.

Language develops to take account of changing political, social, ethical and economic circumstances and so the challenge presented seems glaringly obvious. Author and speaker Martin Scott in his essay, 'The Redemptiveness of Male Imagery', comments, 'Terminology can at times be unhelpful and perhaps it is time to seek new terminology that will help communicate the truths of scripture within our culture.' [21] He continues by provoking us to 'be more open to using "she" when appropriate as the masculine pronoun often now carries exclusive connotations.' [21]

This healthy willingness to remove linguistic obstacles from those seeking the spiritual is refreshing and long overdue. It also positions a love for humanity higher up the list of essentials than a love for tradition. Pursuing tradition simply for the sake of it will eventually turn churches into museums, content to be purveyors of 'apparently' beautiful language but tragically empty of meaning, relevance and application.

> **god is the true father and true mother of all natural things – mother julian of norwich** [22]

To view God as neither male nor female, but to comprehend that God is both Father and Mother will be one of the biggest cultural shifts of the new century. Gender-biased language will have to be challenged and no longer accommodated, with an emphasis upon inclusive language at the forefront of communication.

To view God as neither male nor female, but to comprehend that God is both Father and Mother will be one of the biggest cultural shifts of the new century.

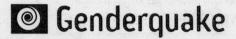 Genderquake

the third sex

> although we tend to think that human beings come in two kinds, male and female, the reality is actually a little more complicated – **simon andreae** [1]

Foetal development is as intricate as it is miraculous. Early into the journey after conception, Andreae explains that each individual has a

> dual set of tiny undeveloped tubes which will become either the sperm ducts or the fallopian tubes, and a little clump of ambiguous cells which will become either the scrotum and penis, or the vagina and clitoris. Should this state of affairs continue into the sixth or seventh week, with no input from any hormonal substances, the foetus will develop along female lines and be born as a little girl. However, should the foetus be flooded with testosterone, the genitals, body and brain will divert themselves from the typical female path and follow the male one instead. [1]

Like all complicated procedures, natural or otherwise, there is room for error. If there are irregularities in the amount of testosterone released, then the effect can be drastic upon the developing child. Some male babies are unable to produce the testosterone which helps external male genitals to develop, and if this is the case, they are born with the 'internal reproductive organs of a boy but the external genitals of a girl. Should a female foetus produce too much testosterone, the child will have the internal reproductive organs of a girl but external genitals which more closely resemble those of a boy.' [1]

In the Dominican Republic, cases of a 'third sex' were identified in the early seventies. [2] It raises a whole host of questions relating to sex and gender. With no medical intervention, would a child develop a male gender identity despite having been brought up a girl?

Public awareness of gender ambiguities is more heightened than ever before. In the US and Europe, medically correcting the ambiguous genitalia of intersexed children began in the late 1950s and this has caused huge debate over whether one's gender identity is biologically determined or shaped by culture. Is it nature or nurture? There are over two thousand surgeries performed each year in the US, assigning a sex to those who are intersex. [2]

Is it nature or nurture?

joel to joella

Joel was born with severe abdominal abnormalities and no formed sexual organs. Life expectancy was considered to be very short and so the parents rushed to get the child baptised and chose a male name. The baby miraculously lived on, and doctors advised that the only hope of Joel leading a normal life was as a female. The parents had to decide what sex to make their child. [3]

Accepting medical advice, Joel underwent surgery to make her look female and subsequently Joel became Joella. Ten years later, after much campaigning, the birth certificate was changed enabling Joella legally to be considered female, and enabling her to marry.

Sexual limbo is not comfortable territory and more people than ever seem to be there.

> **Sexual limbo is not comfortable territory and more people than ever seem to be there.**

ambiguous

As a rule, human beings prefer the predictability of conformity. If it moves, define it and label it. We can feel uncomfortable and insecure with the unknown, the unsure and the odd. A challenge to our comfort zones can induce fear and discrimination. Certainly those who are sexually ambiguous possess the potential to threaten.

Post-modern society has made great strides towards accepting the ambiguous at a certain level. This is partly due to the fashion of androgyny, based upon the anything-goes school of philosophy. Calvin Klein adopted the androgynous look within his advertising and brought it to the attention of the world. By using models to flaunt androgyny, transvestites to sell jeans and by challenging stereotypical sexual image, a mark of acceptability has been granted. The future, people say, is a-gender, with the blurring of sexual and gender distinctions sanctioned as normal and gender disruption is now just another entertainment strategy.

Many may welcome the challenge to conformity, but genuine sexual dysphoria is far more serious. It is not a fashion accessory, it cannot be captured within a fragrance or a clever slogan. It goes much deeper.

We can feel uncomfortable and insecure with the unknown, the unsure and the odd. A challenge to our comfort zones can induce fear and discrimination.

in the wrong body

> i don't want to go through surgery, but i have to. if i don't, i will probably go mad. my male physique is a deformity, i just want to be normal – **a transsexual's story** [4]

Transgenders are a broad alliance of people who are 'inclined to cross the gender line'. [2] Zachary I. Nataf, a transgender activist explains, 'It includes cross-dressers and transvestites as well as intersex people and transsexuals – both those who have and have not had "gender" realignment. Transsexuals whose gender identity is in conflict with their birth gender usually want to achieve a congruence of identity, role and anatomy by having sex-reassignment surgery.' [2]

Not all transsexuals have surgery, some come 'out' as a transsexual and live their life in keeping with what they believe is their core gender identity. For their honesty, all they get is abuse, ridicule, alienation and distress in return. However, in Britain those who do have surgery are legally bound by the term 'boy' or 'girl' written on their birth certificate. Although many have campaigned for transsexuals to be liberated from this birth description and have appealed to the European Charter of Human Rights, they have been turned down. Consent, though, is only a matter of time.

Recent research has suggested that in one foetus in every ten thousand, an area of the brain responsible for gender develops in contradiction with the external sex organs. Some seven thousand patients have undergone surgery in Britain, and two-thirds went from a male to a female identity. [4]

sex and gender

Sex is not gender. Sex is biological and gender is social, cultural, psychological and historical. Certain behavioural patterns, predetermined roles in society, domestic responsibilities, acceptable careers, the way a person looks and dresses – all this is contained within the person's gender which is usually assigned at birth along with the sex.

gender stereotyping

> males are generally seducers and females the seduced. in the matter of seduction, it is the male who is expected to make the first move. women may flirt, but men pounce – **matt ridley, *the red queen*** [5]

Historically, boys have been labelled 'the provider', 'the warrior', whereas girls have been considered 'maternal' and 'domestic'. All this can be true of course, but the boxes which have been used to define gender roles have recently come under well-deserved heavy scrutiny. They have been declared so restrictive and claustrophobic that if an individual doesn't fit into the box, they feel a misfit, an oddity.

> although our culture is rather resistant to the image of the non-nurturant woman, some of us feel we are not interested or cut-out to be mothers – **our bodies ourselves** [6]

There is a theory about the two sides of the brain: one side is creative and intuitive, the other is logical and pragmatic. Women were born with the first half and men with the second. This has long been used to substantiate why women are the best at looking after the home, the children and the cooking, whilst men go to work and make the business decisions. It's strange how the cooking is so often left to the women in the home situations, yet most chefs who appear on the numerous television programmes which grace our screens, are men! Except of course the male domain of 'the barbecue', when hubby charcoals the sausages and bravely endures the smoke and the heat.

I remember my days at school, when the choice for the girls was between needlework or domestic science and for the boys, technical drawing or metalwork. I was never any good at needlework and failed to see the importance of making my own pin cushion! Thankfully, all that has changed and there is now equal choice for girls and boys. We now have an educational system where, on the whole, the girls are outstripping the boys as well as being more attentive in lessons. Girls are not only doing well in the creative subjects, but in mathematics and sciences, going on to take jobs in accountancy and engineering, previously considered logical vocations. So why are the girls on top?

Julie Burchill comments,

> a reasonable explanation is that, because real education was so new to girls, they simply tried harder and finally, in the eighties, caught and overtook the complacent, confident boys in a classic tortoise-and-hare scenario. It is not castrating feminism that now sees boys falling behind girls on every educational level, but rather the culmination of centuries of male supremacy which taught them that, without trying, they will do better than their sisters at school and that the plum pickings of the job market will forever be reserved for them, solely because of the shape of their genitals.[7]

Strong words, softly spoken. But it does seem to make sense that men and women, imprisoned by gender stereotypes, simply conform to conditioned expectations and behaviour. For some it works, but many are screaming to be released from the historical boxes which have confined and disfigured them, and to be released to be themselves, to follow their own instincts and inclinations.

> **if boys are to be contenders again, they will get there by feeling oppressed and becoming determined, disciplined and self-reliant, as both girls and ethnic minority children have had to before them – julie burchill** [7]

... the boxes which have been used to define gender roles have recently come under well-deserved heavy scrutiny.

plastic icons

Mattel Inc. have a lot to answer for. The power of the boardroom executives, fuelled by the smell of money, has wielded a surprising influence over the generations. The seven-inch plastic Barbie doll has reinforced the image that to be truly feminine, you have to be curvy, glam and blonde. Her wardrobe is fem, furs and pink, and her shoes must be stilettos. The pressure to conform to this image of 'feminine' has been immense. Those who cannot or will not fall in line with this stereotype have had to live with feelings of a low self-worth and suffer the consequences.

We see this stereotypical image strengthened as yet another 'blonde woman on television' appears on our screens as the latest game show co-presenter or chat show host. Even a lack of talent does not displace them. I am sure the 'powers that be' feel that womankind will be pleased to see jobs not always going to the boys, but they fail to realise that they have fallen foul of something much worse: *tokenism*. It may not be jobs for the boys, but it is jobs for the girls that the boys fancy! Since when have big breasts been the deciding factor upon which to commission a television series? Given a choice, we would prefer intelligent questioning and on screen appeal, regardless of looks. After all, there are a lot of not-so-good looking men on TV! One can only hope that the situation will change when more egalitarian conscious people make programmes.

The Fluffragettes recently tried to make an impression with their 'fluffy manifesto'. Aiming to put the 'femininity back into feminism', they set the following as their goals: don't contradict a man, even when he's wrong; never be strident or aggressive; flutter your eyelashes; speak softly, don't shriek; think kindly of men; and never mention the f-word. Harping back to the early 1950s, their manifesto did not win many votes, but they will always be with us.

Men can also feel pressurised into displaying cultural stereo-typical 'masculine' traits. So they force back the tears in public, desperately trying not to show their sensitive side, and definitely do not own up to liking cross-stitch. The 'Action Man' image seems far more appropriate. In fact, society has denied men the opportunity of being whole; to be honest about their feelings, to cry, to look after the baby, to experience deep companionship, in fact to enjoy and utilise the full extent of who they are. Cultural expectations have driven him to succeed, to compete and to achieve. This has caused major stress for those men who cannot live up to these expectations. Society needs the liberation of men as well as the liberation of women.

It may not be jobs for the boys, but it is jobs for the girls that the boys fancy!

masculine and feminine

If there is one battle-cry worth shouting it is 'stop boxing me in'. The terms 'masculine' and 'feminine' are constantly in use and yet how often do we analyse what we really mean by them? In this radical age, people are questioning; inquisitive about what defines them and how they are defined. Restless in their pilgrimage for reality, truth and community, everything is under the spotlight.

Elaine Storkey in *The Search for Intimacy* writes, 'There is the assumption that we all know what is meant by masculinity and femininity and that these are universal biological attributes. But they are gender characteristics that vary widely from society to society. The hand-holding and fondling behaviour of African Bangwa men would be seen as perfectly "masculine" in that culture.' [8]

Storkey continues by saying that these gender differences are primarily cultural. There are studies which have investigated the biological differences based upon anatomy and different hormone levels, and there is evidence of physiological differences, but 'the differences between men and women's brain hemispheres simply does not account for the size of the discrepancies which actually exist in work patterns in society'. [8]

Why, for example, is football considered a man's game? In 1921, the Football Association banned women from playing in football league grounds, saying, 'The game is quite unsuitable for females and ought not to be encouraged.' [9] Needless to say, those in authority were probably all male and they wished to continue to dominate a thriving game that would generate a large amount of money for those involved. Yet women's football is the largest growing sport in England and the FA are looking to develop a scheme where young women can study and play football. But the day when it is recognised in the same way as men's football seems a long way off, if it arrives at all.

> If there is one battle-cry worth shouting it is 'stop
> boxing me in'.

promise keepers

> men are weeping openly in the pews, men who ain't
> supposed to cry unless their team has won the
> super bowl. but here they are, middle-age guys
> sobbing and hugging – *time* magazine [10]

Promise Keepers is a movement committed to calling men to take
'spiritual leadership' over their wives. Their philosophy suggests
that American men face a moral and spiritual crisis and its founder
Bill McCartney believes that a man's spiritual make-up differs
from a woman's and that men need a 'masculine context that
allows them to come clean'. McCartney defines Promise Keepers
as a 'Christ-centred ministry dedicated to uniting men through
vital relationships to become godly influences in their world'. [10]

There are mixed feelings about this expanding Promise Keepers
movement, which has a base in England. Some view it as a
regression to the days of male supremacy, and Patricia Ireland,
president of the National Organisation of Women, comments,
'Two adults standing as equals and peers taking responsibility for
their family is a much different image than the man being the head
and master, and women being back in an old role that historically
was very detrimental.' [10]

It is also close to the message of Protestant Fundamentalist
preachers in the US in the early 1900s. In 'Marriage, Obedience
and Feminine Submission', Myfanwy Franks writes, 'Billy Sunday,
in reaction against the feminisation of religion, took a theological
approach and emphasised the masculinity of God. Sunday told his

congregation that Christianity was not "a pale, effeminate proposition, but the robust, red blooded faith of Jesus". This was known as muscular Christianity.' [11]

Others see it as an excellent opportunity for men to be honest within a same-sex environment about their transgressions, dedicating themselves to the promise of taking responsibility in the church, in families, in the community and in the workplace. Each rally, held in various stadiums around the US, has averaged 50,000 men.

Movements such as Promise Keepers are predictably evolving at a time when society is redefining gender and culture. Faith, and one's perspective of God, is very much part of the discussion. Women-only rallies are also taking place, focusing on the issues and responsibilities of being a Christian woman.

Same-sex gatherings do have a place, but there are also dangers involved. Heresy is truth taken to the extreme, and perhaps in emotion-charged rallies, there can be the risk of extremism. There can also be the risk of leadership 'spiritualising' their cultural preferences and indoctrinating new generations with the same historical prejudice as their own. Is this progress?

A more challenging and prophetic scene would surely be gatherings that contain both sexes, with contributions from women and men, and with those attending having the freedom totally to be themselves: expressing emotion, comment, opinion without defensiveness, forging a way forward together. *That* would be progress.

> i long for the day when gender becomes invisible to both men and women, when we are able to work in the partnership and complementarity that god intended and when what qualifies a person for a job is their gifts and calling, not their gender
> – **jenny baker** [12]

Movements such as Promise Keepers are predictably evolving at a time when society is redefining gender and culture.

being real

Real people defy generalisation. Men and women, free from cultural restraint and learned behaviour, are possibly more alike than opposite. If both sexes learn to view each other on that basis then maybe women are from Jupiter, and so are men!

Men and women both share a capacity for pain, love, relationship, justice, sensation, tenderness; and I hope that the future world allows men and women to explore all those characteristics amidst a common framework of community and respect.

men are mothers too

> the plain fact is that one in five women in developed countries like britain is living out her adult life without bearing a child – **joan smith** [13]

It has only recently become acceptable for a woman to choose whether or not to have a child without a negative stigma being attached to that decision. Joan Smith, in her book *Different for Girls: How Culture Creates Women*, explains, 'For centuries, childlessness in women was a curse, even though childbirth was at best painful and at worst fatal. Yet women everywhere dreaded the discovery that they were barren.' [13]

The maternal instinct was considered to be integral to being a woman, and no consideration was given to the possibility that some women would like the choice not to become a mother. Even

153

birth control was concerned with 'regulating the number of children individual women gave birth to, rather than the heretical notion that contraception might give them a choice not to have any at all', comments Smith. [13]

Social change has moved this debate on a long way. Assumptions of what a woman should achieve in life have shifted, particularly in western culture. It is acceptable to choose a career path, to choose to remain single, to choose to be financially independent, to choose possibly to start a family later on in life, and still be a natural woman. The Office for National Statistics has predicted that the proportion of women not ever having children 'has increased sharply over time and it is now expected that over a fifth of women born in 1967 will still be childless when they reach 40'.

It is also possible for a couple having a child to plan for the man to stay at home whilst the woman continues with her career, without prejudice and discriminatory comments. This would have been unthinkable a few decades ago, and yet is now a sensible decision if the woman either has better financial or career path opportunities, or if the man prefers to give his whole attention to the maternal instincts within his character. Surely the woman does not have the monopoly on nurturing and developing a child? Strange as it may seem to some people, there are far more men standing outside the school gates than ever. There is also the possibility of job-sharing, so that the couple can share the role of parenting.

These changing patterns are reflecting the turbulence within a society that is abandoning stereotypical conformity in search of equality. There will always be those who keep a tight grasp on 'the ways of history' and there will always be surveys to authenticate their thinking. However, we have all witnessed enough decon-struction and if the new millennium is to be any different from the past, it has got to embrace the concept of choice and construct new models based upon equality, community and partnership.

for every woman who is tired of acting weak when
    she knows she is strong,
there is a man who is tired of appearing strong
    when he feels vulnerable;
for every woman who is tired of acting dumb,
there is a man who is burdened by the constant
    expectation of 'knowing everything';
for every woman who is tired of being called an
    emotional female,
there is a man who is denied the right to weep and
    be gentle;
for every woman who is called unfeminine when she
    competes,
there is a man for whom competition is the only way
    to prove his masculinity;
for every woman who is tired of being a sex object,
there is a man who must worry about his potency;
for every woman who feels 'tied down' by her
    children,
there is a man who is denied the pleasure of shared
    parenthood;
for every woman who is denied meaningful
    employment or equal pay,
there is a man who must bear the full responsibility
    for another human being;
for every woman who was not taught the intricacies
    of an automobile,
there is a man who was not taught the satisfaction
    of cooking;
for every woman who takes a step towards her own
    liberation,
there is a man who finds the way to freedom has
    become a little easier

nancy r. smith

> ... if the new millennium is to be any different from the
> past, it has got to embrace the concept of choice and
> construct new models based upon equality, community
> and partnership.

the challenge

> according to the 'delivering for women: progress so
> far' think-tank, an organisation committed to
> radical thinking, 90's britain is being shaped by
> feminine values. over a quarter of all women say
> they feel part of a world spirit, and values such as
> environmentalism, empathy and care are now
> central to british society. how can women be so
> powerful and yet so powerless? to have the
> confidence to stride successfully through life,
> young women need not just good role models, but
> encouragement and information from an early age.
> perhaps the time has come for a radical rethink of
> what is taught in schools — and how
> — daniela soave, who do you think you are?
> *scene* magazine, jan/feb 1999

After years of male domination, the pendulum was bound to swing. Women have found their voice, and with the aid of education, medicine and perseverance, the situation seems to be in reverse. It is now the men who feel redundant, endangered, threatened and superfluous to requirements.

Radical feminist, Shulamith Firestone, proclaimed that the reproductive technology of the future would hold the key to women's freedom. Firestone, a founder of the liberation movement in the sixties, said in her book *The Dialectic of Sex* that 'women must be freed from the tyranny of their biology by any means available'. [14] However, I cannot imagine that she envisioned the future to look like it does.

Modern embryology and scientific technology can create life without the need for a sexual relationship with a man. Same sex female couples can be classified as 'family' and the campaign for being an independent woman has appeared successful! The challenge to men is immense.

The Family Futures Report, commissioned by Barclays Life, says,

> women will become better educated and earn more than ever before, while men will opt out of office life in large numbers, choosing to work from home. Not only will women of 2020 be able to command the same salaries as men, they will lay down the law when it comes to duties at home. Post 2020, women may actually earn more than men as their flexibility and organisational skills prove more attractive to employers. [15]

The report predicts a phenomenon of 'downshifting dads – around 20 per cent of fathers will stay at home to work on the computer and in the kitchen. Men will be more appreciated for their fatherly skills and will take more interest in the education and upbringing of their offspring.' [15]

I hope this current situation will not aggravate men into clawing back the power. Otherwise we will watch a rerun of history, this time at a faster, more dangerous pace. There has been such a process of learning and re-education, that men and women may eventually face one another as equals, with more in common than originally thought. Respect.

It is now the men who feel redundant, endangered, threatened and superfluous to requirements.

👤 Single Minded

the plot so far ...

> singles are not regarded as individuals, but as 50 per cent of a potential couple — **marcus berkmann** [1]

How many times have you heard, 'I can't understand why she's still single ... she's so attractive!'? Thought to be affirming and comforting words, instead they succeed only to patronise. Since when has beauty been a criterion for marriage?

Consider the labels that have stuck to single people like candy floss to a child: second class, half a person, unfulfilled, lonely, failure; or consider these well-worn phrases: 'something must be wrong with him' or 'she's just too fussy'.

Living with these labels firmly fastened to your persona is not an easy task for anyone to grapple with so it is not surprising that many single people have felt the pressures and stigma surrounding their lifestyle of solo-ness to be just too enormous to face. Being single has, until very recently, gone against the cultural norm. As a result, many have conceded to become fully paid up members of the *left on the shelf club*, or *social lepers* subjected to probing questions, or followers of the 'desperate and dateless' events featured in their local newspaper's 'what's on' column.

Consider the labels that have stuck to single people like candy floss to a child.

singleness vs celibacy

> celibacy isn't as good as good sex — but it's a lot better than bad sex — **mark edwards**
>
> celibacy has its native country in heaven. here below it is like a stranger: in heaven it is at home — **ambrose, fourth century**

So what does single mean? Answers in word association exercises include, 'one alone', 'unwanted', 'free', 'young' and the *Oxford Dictionary* definition is 'one only, not double, one by itself, unmarried, lonely, unaided'. In practice, singles are a diverse group and the label can include those who have never married with no sexual experience, as well as those with a history of cohabiting or other sexual relationships. It can include those who are lone parents, or those who are now separated, divorced or widowed. Some are single by choice and opt for voluntary singleness, whereas others are single by circumstance or social reasons and find themselves recipients of involuntary singleness.

Celibacy on the other hand is all about chastity, purity and virginity and describes those who abstain from sexual intercourse. The word 'celibacy' has historically caused people to think immediately of nuns and monks. Some people choose the way of chastity as a lifetime commitment, whereas others opt for a specific period of celibacy for varying reasons.

life to the max

> the hardest time of the day for any normal single
> person is between 10 p.m. and a.m. when we
> presume much of humanity is enjoying sex – **anon**
>
> single adults are intimacy starved rather than
> sexually deprived – **elaine storkey** [2]

Whether an individual is single for a short while or for a lifetime, or whether the single life is one of choice or circumstance, it is questionable whether living as a single person is ever adequately dialogued or explored. There are a multiplicity of pressures that face single people socially and sexually. Also, being single at forty years old is very different from being single at twenty. Dialogue and interaction are especially important in discussing and trying to come to terms with these pressures, especially for those who may feel that they have been called to celibacy for life, for whatever reason. There are many elements of singleness that are helpful to discuss but one of the most crucial is the whole arena of sexual pressure.

Sexual images and adventures bombard us from every angle. If we are to believe the 'bump 'n' grind' stimuli of music and the bodytalk of videos, then we believe that in order to be fully alive one has to be fully sexually active. Romance surrounds us, the 'couple syndrome' often dominates social etiquette and condom machines stare at us from most public conveniences! The more sexually experienced we are, then the more advanced our character and the more exciting our journey of life. Even Barbie craves some 'hanky panky', as featured in the pop song by Aqua! This global message of hormonal happiness poses a crisis for the single person not in a sexual relationship, who is left to feel alienated and abnormal. Does this mean that if you are single then you are non-sexual and living on an inferior parallel universe? Is the non-sexual single person to be pitied or admired? Are they to be envied for their freedom or suspected for posing a potential threat to existing couples?

How many MTV videos can a single person sit through before reaching for the off button? How many Celine Dion love songs amount to overload?

By the very nature of being sexually inactive, are single people or those who are celibate therefore non-sexual? Is a volcano still a volcano even if it is dormant …? Of course it is. In the same way it is evident that single people actually do have a sexuality, even if one expression of it lies dormant. It all depends upon one's definition of sexuality. Our orgasm-orientated world has narrowed the definition to mean that sexuality is directly linked to being sexually active. But if you take a more holistic view, sexuality is all about expressing who we are, our personality, character, image, and not solely our biological anatomy and usage of that anatomy. Sexuality is not wrapped up in belonging to one person and being single does not mean therefore that the individual is non-sexual. Society has 'sexualised' sexuality and attached an automatic orgasm-obsession to it.

Elaine Storkey in her book, *The Search for Intimacy*, affirms 'only one aspect of our sexuality is expressed in sexual intercourse. We can also express it in warmth and touch, in closeness and care for the other persons who are dear to us. If in our lives there is no sexual union with another, we are no less fully human and fully sexual.' [3]

Society has 'sexualised' sexuality and attached an automatic orgasm-obsession to it.

a sense of belonging

> you know the song — 'you're nobody until somebody loves you'? Well, I was 26 and I'd never been in love; not truly in love. I was single, never married, a nobody — **kate jackson, _you_ magazine** [4]

We are still living in the aftermath of the global marriage culture which has connected self-worth and value with belonging to someone in marriage or in partnership. If you do not belong to anyone in a specific way, then by default you are classified as a nobody. Once upon a time, if a woman was still single after thirty she would have failed both herself and her family.

As Ian Stuart Gregory writes in _No Sex Please, We're Single_, 'A generation ago we were still very much a male dominated society. And in patriarchies where power is in male hands, it is imperative for a woman to be linked with a man in marriage.' [5]

The marriage covenant is an excellent and honourable journey for two people to follow together for life, but unfortunately one of the side effects has been the implication that if you are not in a 'relationship' or if you are not married, then you are obviously not worth loving and probably difficult to live with! Countless single people have no doubt asked themselves the same burning question, 'What is wrong with me?' as they sit through yet another wedding ceremony wondering what the bride and groom have that they don't have. Valentine's Day can also be a challenge as you watch yet another advert selling chocolates for the 'woman in your life'. Advert number seven proves to be the toffee that sticks in your throat as you glance at the cardless environment of your room and try to convince yourself that the post is often late!

It is easy for single people to become obsessed with being part of a couple and to see this blissful state through romance-coloured spectacles. A 1990 newspaper article entitled 'Two's company, one's an outcast' only served to deepen the pain especially when it stated so audaciously, 'Singles are the new social lepers; barred from couple dominated dinner parties; humiliated at company social functions and subjected to probing questions from suspicious aunts.' [1]

It can easily be forgotten that although there may be loneliness in being single, there can also be loneliness within marriage.

It is easy for single people to become obsessed with being part of a couple.

the changing story

> she's attractive, she's bright, she's successful. so why is this woman and thousands like her – single – *options* magazine
>
> a 90's phenomenon. independent, unattached and loving it. it's hip to be single – *elle* magazine [6]

Now for the good news ... times are changing. Society is radically rethinking singleness in the light of the rapid increase in the single population and the diversity within it. Today more than one in three British adults is single, pushing the singles population to over eighteen million. By 2001, the prediction is that 44 per cent of the adult population will be single. In 2011, there will be three times as many singles as in 1971. [7]

Articles are appearing in contemporary magazines with titles like, 'The Singles Epidemic',[7] 'It's Hip To Be Single' and 'Strong, Happy and Single'. [8] The singleton no longer needs to feel ashamed about her/his status or dream up stories of a partner to impress work colleagues. It is now officially trendy to be single and increasingly credible to be celibate. There's never been a better time to be single. What has caused this extraordinary sea-change within society?

This definite shift reveals the discovery of 'choice' and recognises too the growing number of lone parents. According to Dr Maryon Tysoe, author of the *Good Relationships Guide*, 'The biggest shift in attitude has come from women. These days, many more have financial autonomy and don't need to stay in an unsatisfactory relationship in the way their mother's generation did. Women are also leaving childbirth until later and choose to get their careers off the ground first.' [7]

Statistics do show that people are marrying later in life, therefore pushing up the numbers of single people. Another possible reason could be the pessimism about marriage – there are just too many bad examples! A recent Mintel survey found that most single people are happy that way and, while 30 per cent cite loneliness as a drawback, 53 per cent say that living alone gives them a sense of achievement and 60 per cent say they enjoy their freedom. [7]

As the number of single people rises, the biggest increase is among affluent men and women under the age of thirty-five who have never married. This means that the consumer power of single people is increasingly impressive and the advertising and marketing moguls have quickly caught on to this new era. Nearly two-thirds of single women and 54 per cent of single men are in the more affluent sociodemographic groups, with the result that manufacturers are keen to cater for their needs. Hence the introduction of new style and exotic ready meals for one, as well as the popular Hovis half-loaf. Wandering around the local supermarket can now be liberating for the singleton as there is a healthy alternative to the 'family-size' lasagnes! Apparently some supermarkets even hold 'singles nights' and, although being handed a carnation as you walk through the door may be embarrassing, it is comforting to know that an attempt is being made.

The growing number of single people has also led to a noticeable leisure boom. With around eight hours more leisure time per week than couples, they go out more and that means more spending on cinemas, theatres, restaurants, pubs and exhibitions. Singles holidays are also promoted and noticeably free from the stigma which was once attached to these unloved but available holidaymakers.

> 6 myths of being single – car mechanics rip you off, it's dangerous to be home alone, if the lights fuse it'll be dark until a man arrives, i can't sort out my own finances, two can live as cheaply as one, i'm bound to be mugged without a man by my side – *cosmopolitan*, october 1998 [8]

the interview

Linda Harding worked in the National Health Service for twenty years, first in speech therapy and later in general management and marketing. She left in 1992 to work as a communications consultant, working with a number of organisations on issues relating to PR and communications. Much of her time is spent travelling, giving advice and pastoral care to churches, and lecturing. She has also written a book called *Better Than or Equal To?* which gives insight into being single. [9]

What does being single mean to you?

Freedom to go where I want to go and to be who I want to be! That sounds really selfish but with the freedom comes a responsibility to use my time and my energies to serve God and other people. The challenge

165

is to model that it is possible to be fulfilled without a marriage partner, that I am a whole not half a person, that I am able to form relationships, that I am capable of loving and of being loved, and that I can create home and family.

What do you see regarding singleness in society?

Society is definitely more accepting of single people now than ten years ago. I have experienced changing attitudes and a greater level of understanding. However, at times I still find I am regarded as abnormal or inferior especially as I have never been married. Friends and work colleagues assume I have been married or in a sexual partnership and I am viewed as something of a freak or with suspicion for being celibate. I think it has been more acceptable to have once been married or in a sexual partnership than to always have been single. But in recent years attitudes from married people seem to have changed from feelings of pity to that of envy, and I have even received admiration from married friends who wished they'd had the courage to stay single! This is definitely a change from ten years ago when I was clearly regarded as someone to feel sorry for.

Have you chosen to be single?

Yes I have chosen to be single. It feels like a series of stages and certain birthdays have been landmarks. I made a clear choice when I was twenty-seven to only consider the option of marriage to someone with the same values. I have received some proposals of marriage but can honestly say that none of them attracted me to the prospect of a lifetime commitment ... to say yes would have meant restriction for me. When I was thirty I realised that this choice drastically narrowed my options and that the possibility of getting married was slim! I think for the next few years I lived a day at a time, trying to make the most of my freedom for as long as it lasted. There was however one specific time in my mid-thirties when I faced the challenge to consider the permanence of singleness as a specific calling … it was not an easy decision to make, and I gave it a lot of thought but I have continued to live with this sense of calling. I am not saying I will never marry, someone would have to trip me up, 'cos I'm not looking! Then I would have to consider it very seriously and it would mean a radical change.

What are some of the advantages and disadvantages of being single?

The greatest advantage I enjoy is the freedom, the greatest disadvantage is the loneliness. Being single doesn't mean I have less capacity to give and receive love, but it is not just focused on one person. Having friends of both genders, both adults and children, is an essential not just for survival but to ensure that I don't become self-centred. I am grateful to have a female companion with whom to share my home, and share good times and bad times. This provides a positive opportunity to enjoy companionship, but I have to face the negatives of misunderstanding from those who would want to add the label of lesbian to our friendship.

My conscious decision as a Christian not to have a sexual relationship outside of marriage, has been really difficult at times. I enjoy intimacy and touch, but it has forced me to face up to my own sexuality, to realise I am still a sexual being and I have to find ways of expressing my sexuality, and coping with my sexual needs and desires.

Have you a comment on the meaning of singleness for you in your stage of life?

Being single in my forties is so different from in my twenties or thirties. I have experienced the pain of never having children of my own and yet within the church family discovering the privilege and responsibility of enjoying other people's children. I have had to face the possibility of old

167

age with no natural children to care for me. But as I am getting older there is less pressure now from others to get married or find a partner and I have found friends, family and I think society to be more accepting of me as an older single woman.

It is now officially trendy to be single and increasingly credible to be celibate.

choosing chastity [10]

> i have a sense more people are turning to it though they still find it hard to talk about it – **sally cline** [11]
>
> do not conform to the pattern of the world ... don't become so well adjusted to your culture that you fit into it without thinking. instead fix your attention on god – **romans 12:1, the bible, *message* version** [12]

Celibacy is going through a redemptive process. Our inheritance from the 'sexual revolution' had made the very idea, let alone the reality, of celibacy a shock. However, choosing to be celibate is fast becoming a positive decision, almost a trend, and increasingly one to be admired.

This positive voice of celibacy is barely louder than a whisper but is growing into a shout, even though the pressures to explore the sexual rollercoaster still pervade society. An interview with Edwina Currie's daughter concentrated more on the loss of her virginity at fifteen than on her skills as a wanna-be pop star. Regardless of whether or not this was a publicity stunt, the example still highlights the overall preoccupation with sexual conquests. However, a new flow of coverage is being given to stories like 'I'm proud to be a virgin' and 'No sex please … we're women of the nineties'.[12] Still in the minority but causing waves of support from people for many different reasons. 'The General Household Survey' interestingly reveals that four out of ten single women between sixteen and forty-nine are choosing celibacy. [13]

What is causing people to abstain? Perhaps it's the fear of AIDS? Perhaps it's the lure of a career which demands a focused commitment? Perhaps it's the liberation of women which has revealed that there is more to life than marriage and babies? Perhaps it's the liberation of men who are now desiring to be domestically responsible and live alone rather than seek out a 'mother-figure' in the shape of 'wifey'? Perhaps the 'Hollywood' has gone out of the physical act – an idealism that has portrayed lovemaking or more accurately sex making, as movie-perfect every time with satin sheets and a beautiful string quartet playing by your bedside!

Another reason why people are choosing to abstain is because of a deep faith-driven belief in purity and that sexual intercourse is for marriage only. A new biblical generation of people is emerging with a white hot morality that flows against the tide. There is a thirst for a framework of morality within which to live, and this has only been heightened by the extreme restlessness and pain that has been experienced by moral freedom. Some are choosing lifelong celibacy, preferring to devote their energy and resources to help shape a better world. Others are owning up to the fact that they consider virginity to be precious and worth preserving for the moment when or if they exchange their wedding vows before God and before family and friends.

What a tragic by-product of this disposable age, that thousands throw away their virginity without truly understanding the price. Valuing your God-designed virginity indicates that sexual purity is important to the individual and that sexual intercourse is considered not only a physical act but also a spiritual union.

Celibacy is about freedom. Emphasis should be placed on what you can do, rather than on what you can't. Perhaps a way forward is to encourage celibacy as a positive choice and not a dire consequence, realising that those on this pathway of purity are role models who deserve respect and not ridicule.

the interview

> do not arouse or awaken love until it so desires
> – song of songs 2:7, the bible, niv version

Lucie is seventeen and a student. She has made a conscious choice to wear a ring symbolising purity. In her own words she explains, 'When I was young, I saw the hurt that could come from broken relationships, so I decided not to chase relationships that would be unhelpful. I know that love is complicated but as a Christian, I want to get my attitude right in everything I do. The ring is a symbol of purity, but also of my promise to God and a future husband that I want to honour them with my actions and attitude. Though it seems strange to some people, I can't think of anything more romantic than saving everything that you are for one person. I wear the ring on my wedding finger so that I can make a stand for what I believe in situations where everyone is doing the opposite.'

A new biblical generation of people is emerging with a white hot morality that flows against the tide.

the future is single

> ### the new spinster thrives – **yvonne roberts** [14]
>
> ### they're stylish, ambitious and rich and there are more of them than ever – *independent* [15]

radical family

An area which still needs liberating and developing is 'the family'. Traditionally the word 'family' has included blood and marital relatives. However, this leaves little room for the single person, particularly one who may have little blood family remaining or one who may live miles from their family home. The feelings of alienation and isolation can be overwhelming and surely in the light of the increasing singles' population, there needs to be some enlightenment surrounding the word 'family'.

There are many examples of single people feeling part of a family simply because they have been accepted and embraced, not out of pity but out of genuine appreciation for who they are.

They have influence within the family relationships, they are role models for the children and together radical family can be outworked in an egalitarian and sharing way. Inclusivity based on friendship and appreciation bears fruit not only for the single person, but for each member of the family. It also models to the world something extremely precious and prophetic. Everybody wants and needs somewhere to belong – in fact the desire to belong is central to the heart of humanity – and an inclusive household can provide a homely environment to a variety of people. If this were more prevalent, then maybe there would be a greater sense of community and goodwill and maybe there would be a lot less loneliness.

To live alone is one thing but to be lonely is an entirely different state of affairs – and from this no one is exempt!

companionship

The increase in the singles' population also accounts for more single people living together, not simply as flat-mates or lodgers but as companions. A lot of ground has been won by gay and lesbian campaigners over the years in educating people to value their relationships on an equal footing to those of heterosexual couples. So much so that, as previously mentioned, insurance companies, mortgage companies and the like will now offer the same rights to same-sex partners as they do to opposite-sex partners. However, discrimination now faces an entirely new kind of partnership: a new century model which will only grow in number and will eventually cause companies to rethink their advertising and strategy.

The new partnership is that of two single people living together as companions, sharing a mortgage, sharing the household bills but being discriminated against because they do not share the bed!

For example, travel insurance companies will accommodate partners of the same sex who share a mortgage, share the household bills and have a sexual relationship under their family member advantage schemes but will not accommodate partners of the same sex who share the mortgage, share the household bills but have a purely platonic relationship. In this day and age, who can guarantee which of these two models of partners will be more long lasting? A cry has to go up for 'companionship rights' or 'celibate rights'! There is of course always the temptation to lie and admit to a sexual allegiance in order to get the deal and save money, but that should never be the option to choose.

The future is single, so people say, but also the future is about companionship. It is possible for two individuals to be covenanted together in a platonic way. By 'covenanted' I mean a decision made by two consenting adults to model respect, trust, mutual responsibility, financial commitment and possibly a social calendar under one roof! It is also a relatively long-term but ultimately non-binding agreement.

This 'new partnership' will surely change the negative stigma so often attached to a life of singleness, and living out this model should one day be considered an equal and viable alternative to any other form of commitment.

Society needs to beware of reinventing the wheel. The scenario where the adult or parent puts pressure upon the child to marry, advocating this status to be *the* expected way to go, has really got to be challenged. Singleness should be promoted positively as an equal option. Yes it has many flaws but so does marriage!

This 'new partnership' will surely change the negative stigma so often attached to a life of singleness, and living out this model should one day be considered an equal and viable alternative to any other form of commitment.

☒ Ethics a snapshot

restless times [1]

> the unworthy become rich
> the unhappy become medicated
> and the unheard are asked to choke on their rage
> — anon

We are regularly confronted with newspaper headlines such as 'An abortion in your lunch-hour', and 'Victory for gays as Labour surrenders over the age of consent'. If that were not enough, we are now diving head-first into the huge emotional debate surrounding the legalisation of voluntary euthanasia or 'mercy killing', which could possibly be the issue to split the medical profession. Dr Michael Irwin, a leading figure in this discussion, announced, 'I feel no guilt in helping people die.'

No longer can we hope for these important issues to disappear until a more suitable time, and no longer can we leave the medical profession alone to contend with them. They are firmly positioned within the public arena and we *have* to face them!

There is a strong aroma of new-millennium restlessness which is causing the populous to wrestle with the serious issues of the day. The current social climate seems a fertile environment for these ethical issues to emerge and take shape, encouraging a new form of radicalism. There are no easy answers and the days for trite, passionless and phobic answers are thankfully long gone!

The offer of a ten-minute termination, a walk in and walk out service, has serious repercussions. Even in this disposable, throw-away age who would have imagined that human life could be another commodity so easily extinguishable? Perhaps the psycho-logical damage of a 'lunchtime' termination is not quite so easy to deal with? Many would echo the comments of Nuala Scarisbrick, a Life organisation trustee, who remarked, 'It is a sad statement of how desensitised and dehumanised the abortion trade has become.'[2]

As we surge towards the third millennium, we must keep our focus on the central belief that all human life has value and dignity.

> **The current social climate seems a fertile environment for these ethical issues to emerge and take shape, encouraging a new form of radicalism.**

inside ethics

> ethics: the science of morals, that branch of philosophy which is concerned with human character and conduct: a system of morals, rules of behaviour: a treatise on morals – *chambers english dictionary*

Our ethics form the basis upon which we determine what is right and wrong, and influence the way we choose to live and behave. As we journey through life, invariably blitzed by situations, rela-tionships and dilemmas, we are consistently provoked to evaluate the basis upon which we make choices and why we regard some things as right and others as wrong.

How do we develop personal ethics? We can be deeply

175

influenced by one of the many belief systems, such as Buddhism, or adopt an ethical system based upon human reason. Our ethical stance may be rooted in personal experience and feelings, or it may be formulated by observing other people's experiences. We may have certain personal and global aspirations or an inherent vision of how we perceive humanity should operate. Some may keep the same ethical attitude throughout their lifetime, whereas others adapt and modify over the course of time.

Ethics and morality are not the same. In *Ethics and Belief*, Baelz helpfully writes, 'A moral problem is concerned with right and wrong. Ethics may conveniently be defined as the study of morality. Ethics is a reflective or theoretical business, it steps back from the immediately practical and attempts to discover some underlying pattern or order in the immense variety of moral decisions and practices of both individuals and of societies.' [3]

The Christian heritage of past generations still influences modern thinking, even though people may fail to realise this. The provocation to tell the truth, to keep loyal to your word, to love your neighbour and to value all human life; all have their basis in Christian ethics. Although society has changed considerably and challenged these original Christian values with its adoption of other worldviews, faiths and secular thinking, they still form a bedrock within society.

Whatever the culture, people are fascinated with the concept of right and wrong. The 'moral' dilemma occupies many a conversation, song, magazine quiz and big screen movie. Even large stadium events, supported by top entertainment personalities, are organised to raise awareness and finance to right the wrong of poverty or to support some other 'just' cause. The now infamous 'Live Aid', organised by Bob Geldof, was a forerunner for large 'moral' gatherings, and on that occasion the people's spokesman Geldof urged those trying to explain the malnutrition and suffering of fellow human beings, 'Don't blame God, blame man.'

> a moral life is one of continuous questioning
> – **socrates**

As we journey through life, invariably blitzed by situations, relationships and dilemmas, we are consistently provoked to evaluate the basis upon which we make choices and why we regard some things as right and others as wrong.

community

> my neighbour is no longer just the person next door, rather: the child who made my shoes, the company who makes my breakfast cereal, the multinational that drills for my petrol in ogoni land and the government that takes my taxes and spends them on weapons to kill – **greg valerio, 'where revival and justice meet'** [4]

Personal ethics are constantly tried and tested. The uncertainty of the nineties has brought to the attention of the masses a toxic society in social crisis. The reasons are many, ranging from the breakdown of the family unit, decline in organised religion, the increase in single parent families, post-modern cynicism and the increase in crime, to corruption and 'sleaze' in public life. Individuals have been compelled to examine or ignore their conscience, appraise or neglect their behaviour and choose either to set themselves a framework of values within which to live or opt out of any responsibility whatsoever.

'Be good, be bad, just be' may be successful at selling a 'shared fragrance', but an approach to life based upon 'the gospel according to Klein' has resulted in ethical chaos.

Despite the heavy doses of disillusionment of the nineties Vanessa Baird, in her article 'How Are We To Live?' observes, 'Faced with this general suspension of moral and political responsibility, concerned people want to get a grip on things, want to rescue the idea of "responsibility". The buzzword doing the rounds and inspiring hope is "community". Some see it as a return to community, others as building community.' [5]

Community can be viewed in a variety of ways, from limiting the boundary to a region to widening it extensively to encompass the community of humankind. Peter Singer, one of the world's leading moral philosophers, writes,

> Our century is the first in which it has been possible to speak of global responsibility and a global community. For most of human history, we could affect the people in our village, or perhaps in a large city, but even a powerful King could not conquer far beyond the borders of his kingdom. Instant communications have changed all that. A television audience of two billion people can now watch hungry children beg for food in an area struck by famine. The need for a global ethic is inescapable. [6]

The uncertainty of the nineties has brought to the attention of the masses a toxic society in social crisis.

human rights

No debate about ethics, values or morality would seem complete without pausing for a while to consider the common standard of universally recognised principles to shape a better world. On 10 December 1948, the General Assembly of the United Nations adopted and proclaimed the Universal Declaration of Human Rights.

Fifty-one years on, it still remains a powerful commitment to freedom, respect and dignity and is even more poignant today than ever.

> article 1: all human beings are born free and equal in dignity and rights. they are endowed with reason and conscience and should act towards one another in a spirit of brotherhood
>
> article 2: everyone is entitled to all the rights and freedoms set forth in this declaration, without distinction of any kind, such as race, colour, sex, language, religion, political or other opinion, national or social origin, property, birth or other status
>
> article 4: no one shall be held in slavery or servitude. slavery and the slave trade shall be prohibited in all their forms
>
> article 5: no one shall be subjected to torture or to cruel, inhuman or degrading treatment or punishment

There is an increasing understanding that ethical values are not concerned with sexual matters alone. A *holistic* outlook will conclude that you cannot be ethical in part only, but every element of lifestyle and behaviour should come under the microscope. This holistic approach can be quite daunting, and for many, the commitment required to follow such a path can appear so incredibly absorbing that they reject this course of action. Living ethically is not about existing on some unattainable virtuous dimension. It is simply choosing to be aware, to feel the pain and injustice, to quantify how modern technology affects our environment and decide to contribute something positive on the basis of our reflections and conclusions.

The small world approach to life is hopefully in decline. Many more people are taking a look at the big picture with a desire to discard passivity and participate. Ethics is a boom industry and there is a marked interest in single issue ethics.

> **A holistic outlook will conclude that you cannot be ethical in part only, but every element of lifestyle and behaviour should come under the microscope.**

ethical consumerism

> as consumers we do indeed have some power. we should use it as constructively as we can, opting for the relatively good rather than the absolutely bad products – **david ransom, 'jeans, the big stitch-up'** [7]

The Ethical Consumer states, 'It has become widely accepted that the global economic system should be able to pursue ethical as well as financial goals. In a world where people feel politically disempowered, and where governments are becoming less powerful than corporations, citizens are beginning to realise that their economic vote may have as much influence as their political vote.' [8]

The aim of magazines like *The Ethical Consumer* and ethical consumer research associations is to enable people to assert their ethical values through the market. Information is provided to allow individuals and groups to make decisions based upon their own beliefs, and not simply to be coerced into an uncomfortable and unmeaningful course of action.

Globalisation has made it easy for businesses to relocate production overseas and bypass various environmental and health and safety rules. In order to remain competitive, it has been possible to operate overseas on principles that are far from fair.

People are becoming more aware of the ways in which raw materials are produced and how the item, garment or product is manufactured. Companies and organisations are therefore increasingly careful about the ethical implications of their actions. Nestlé has been the target of consumer interest for a while, since stirring up controversy with the promotion of a breast milk substitute in developing nations. Boycotting Nestlé products was the reaction – a course of action which some followed with limited staying power, whereas others became interested in the problem at such a level that they began to engage with issues of injustice on a greater scale.

The cultivation of cotton, for example, and the manufacturing of jeans in sweatshops has hit headlines of late. We are informed by David Ransom in his article 'Jeans, The Big Stitch-Up' that 'cotton has spread across five per cent of the earth's cultivable surface, invading fertile communities, sucking them dry with irrigation, shrouding them in poison'. [7] The jeans are then stitched together and processed by 'labour camps, anonymous sheds filled with human misery', [7] for a meagre wage. Long hours, child labour and stories of extreme exploitation have seriously marred the image of designer labels. In the case of some companies, many feel that wearing these labels glorifies injustice.

There may not be the *perfect* ethical garment but consumers can disqualify some companies on the grounds of aggressively and almost unashamedly choosing profit above justice. There are some companies, however, who are wanting to put things right and are responding positively to the ethical revolution.

fairtrade

> serious efforts are being made to introduce fairness
> into international trade. these are closely
> associated to the production of high quality
> chocolate. if dissatisfaction grows with the cocoa-
> poor, sugar-heavy candy that 'big chocolate' passes
> off on a public unaware of alternatives, the market
> niche for better quality chocolate will expand. this is
> a win-win scenario; good for farmers, good for
> consumers, good for the ecosystem – **richard swift,
> 'chocolate saves the world'** [9]

Campaigns run by powerful single-issue groups like Friends of the Earth or Greenpeace have been at the forefront of the drive for ethical business. Campaign techniques have involved: consumer boycotts, direct action, letter writing and the production of specialist ethical shopping guides.

The 'Fairtrade mark' has also been introduced to help ensure a better deal for Third World producers. Set up by Oxfam, Christian Aid and others, the Fairtrade Foundation awards the mark when it sees evidence that the producers are receiving a fair price and are being offered a long term trading agreement. The prices paid for these Fairtrade products – coffee, tea, chocolate – are often above market rates to enable producers to invest for the long term and to ensure workers are able to support their households.

eco-pubs

Those with a taste for ethical drinking will be pleased at the opening of organic eco-pubs. Ecowarrior beer or Whole Earth cola are just a couple of the drinks on sale, and nothing is served which does not conform to the pub's strict green standards.

medical ethics

> what we need today are ethics that expand our vision rather than contract it. ethics that look forward rather than backwards, that are equipped to tackle the vital issues. time is running out. this is nowhere more true than in the boom area of genetic engineering – **vanessa baird** [5]

genetics

> the 1990's have become the decade of the gene – **dr patrick dixon** [10]

The world and wonder of genetics may well have been considered a study for scientists only. The majority of people have dismissed it as either too complex to understand, or irrelevant to normal life – until now. Recent events have frightened, astounded and amazed a population who considered human cloning to be the stuff of science fiction or futuristic films. Things are changing extremely fast and the pace of scientific technological advancement is accelerating beyond all speculation.

Paul Johnson, in his essay 'My Fears For Our Future', writes, 'The real work, the dangerous work, is taking place in the labs, and until recently it lacked not only moral respectability but any hope of legal sanction.' [11]

There has been an extensive gathering of knowledge over the

last ten years concerning genes and the potential for genetic engineering. For many years, the ability to clone animals has been evident. There were allegedly 277 attempts of 'reproductive cloning' before Dolly the sheep was cloned. Dolly was born in 1996 and announced in 1997. Dolly had no father, but was created from a scrap of frozen tissue removed from the udder of an adult ewe. Scientists took a single cell from this tissue, removed the genetic material inside and placed it in a hollowed out unfertilised egg taken from another ewe. The egg, fused with electricity and placed in a surrogate mother, grew into an identical copy of its genetic mother. That same year saw the arrival of Polly, a cloned sheep with human genes. The following year Hawaiian scientists cloned mice and then went on to create clones of those clones.

> **Recent events have frightened, astounded and amazed a population who considered human cloning to be the stuff of science fiction or futuristic films.**

human cloning

> identical twins are clones, formed naturally when an embryo splits in the womb. clones can also be formed artificially using genetic material from skin, brain or blood. they are replicas of their 'parents'
> **– david derbyshire** [12]

The 1990 Human Fertilisation and Embryology Act bans 'reproductive cloning' of babies but permits experiments on very early embryos – of less than fourteen days – for research into infertility, congenital disease, miscarriages, contraception and genetic abnormalities. Dr Jacqueline Laing, a specialist in bio-ethics and moral philosophy, comments, 'That first tentative step towards the Brave New World is to become a giant leap, largely because the public has been conditioned to accept what was once unacceptable.' [13]

The December 1998 report from the Human Genetics Advisory Commission and the Human Fertilisation and Embryology Authority recommended using cloning techniques to create embryos and to use them for research into diseases including Parkinson's and some cancers, but these embryos would not be allowed to develop into babies for infertile couples. The clone would never be allowed to develop beyond two weeks, but it could be used to create cells that could be turned into tissue to create 'spare-parts'.

David Derbyshire, in an article about 'spare-part' cloning, explains, 'The nucleus of the cell – which contains the person's complete DNA blueprint – would be inserted into an unfertilised egg to produce a clone embryo. After a few days, the embryo's stem cells would be removed. They could then be grown in a dish, using the relevant hormones to convert them into whatever type of body tissue was required. Scientists have the vision to clone embryos of patients and use these "stem cells" to grow unlimited spare part tissue.' [14]

carbon-copy people

> to order a 'designer baby' from the lab is a concept which fits in well with our increasingly sophisticated and wealthy consumer society. but there may be appalling risks, of which we know nothing yet, to balance these exciting possibilities. and risks have a horrible habit of becoming catastrophic realities when men play god – **paul johnson, 'is this the most dangerous man in britain today?' *daily mail*, Feb 1999**

Critic Mark Nicholls, spokesman for the pressure group MATCH, the Movement Against The Cloning of Humans, says, 'Therapeutic cloning involves the deliberate creation and destruction of tiny human beings and is therefore ethically worse than pregnancy cloning.' [13] Dr Patrick Dixon, who has warned of the dangers of cloning in his book *Futurewise*, added weight to this disapproval by commenting, 'British scientists have constantly told us that human cloning was some distance away and for that reason there was no great urgency to introduce a global ban on the birth of human clones. However, the first birth of human clones could be very soon. We urgently need a biotech summit looking at every aspect of the genetic revolution.' [14]

There was a shocked reaction to the news that South Korean scientists claimed they had created the first human embryo clone. Under Korean law, the embryo had to be destroyed after three days, but the scientists say it could have grown into a healthy baby if it had been implanted in a womb. The Koreans are not the first to claim they have cloned humans.

An American company claimed it had cloned an embryo by inserting human DNA into an empty egg removed from a cow. A biotechnology company took a cell from Dr Jose Cibelli, a research scientist, and combined it with a cow's egg from which the genes had already been removed. The genes activated and the egg began to divide in the normal way up to the thirty-two cell stage and then it was destroyed. This happened in 1995, and news of it was released only in 1998, three years later.

Whether it be human embryos cloned for research or for spare body parts, the temperature is rising fast. Human life has become a commodity, a laboratory creation similar to Mary Shelley's Dr Frankenstein. Reminiscent of Aldous Huxley's *Brave New World*, where cloning was the basis of an offensive society, fiction has become reality and the miraculous creation of human life degraded to a scientific experiment. A major worry is that the experiments carried out *now* will probably only come to light in a few years' time. This information gap is highly alarming.

> if nascent human life can be coldly exploited simply because it's handy and has no parents or anyone else to speak up for it, we must ask: why should science stop there? once the end justifies the means, we are committed to absurd moral conclusions – **dr jacqueline laing** [13]

... fiction has become reality, and the miraculous creation of human life degraded to a scientific experiment.

gattaca

The futuristic and unsettling film *Gattaca* focused on the dilemma of designer babies. The concept of a 'God-child' was considered strange and inferior compared with the 'natural' way of *designing* the baby of your dreams with an inbuilt life expectancy and the ability to eliminate disease and minor deficiencies. The God-child was made to feel 'invalid', a freak of nature, whereas the scientifically designed model was 'valid' and far superior.

The film made two startling comments which left the viewer grappling for wisdom and praying for insight into this fast approaching ethical situation. The first was a quote by Willard Gaylin, 'I not only think we will tamper with Mother Nature, I think Mother wants us to.' The second was the strapline underneath the film title, '*There is no gene for the human spirit.*'

Genetic engineering offers various possibilities which are quite simply mind-blowing. There are huge risks involved when tampering with life creation and the ethical implications of scientific progress must be weighed up before it is really too late. It may be possible to create a physical, anatomical person through cloning, but as *Gattaca* points out, can a human spirit and soul also be scientifically manufactured?

Those who believe in a creative God as the originator of mind, body and soul are deeply questioning the role that science is playing. Paul Johnson comments, 'We do not know what makes the individual, what gives each human being his or her uniqueness. We do not know what relation the individuality of all of us has to our genetic coding.' [11]

Dixon explains, 'The Christian view is that life is a wonderful gift from God and human beings are his design, in his own image. We have been given the ability to learn about and control our world, but not the authority to destroy it or alter our own nature fundamentally.'[15] Should science play God? Do the advantages of possibly eliminating a whole range of degenerative disorders outweigh the nightmarish repercussions of entering unknown territory?

The notion of 'designer babies' will appeal to many who wish to acquire children immune to a wide range of diseases and imperfections. There will, of course, be a price to pay, but I suspect many will consider it money well spent. In this present age, there appears an insatiable desire to get the latest model of all sorts of 'gadgets' considered necessary for living in the modern world. I fear that designer babies may crudely become one of the latest *gadgets*, acquired over the Internet or through mail order catalogues by answering a simple questionnaire and supplying a credit card number. This technological market-place will be driven by demand and the ability to pay, as humankind begins to take control over its own evolution.

In the words of Dr Laing, 'We may discover one day that we have strayed into a moral wilderness from which there is no escape.' [13]

> human life has become a commodity to be used or abused. the embryos engineered by cloning will have no mother, no father, no status whatever in society. they will enjoy no concept of parentage, no notion of heritage or ancestry. they will simply be material for laboratory use – **dr jacqueline laing** [13]

Those who believe in a creative God as the originator of mind, body and soul are deeply questioning the role that science is playing.

abort?

> a growing number of courageous young doctors are refusing, on grounds of conscience, to perform these operations. this revolt of the young, is not confined to roman catholics. protestants, moslems, jews and non-believers alike are all involved in a deeply moral revolution in attitudes towards the unborn – **dr tony cole, consultant paediatrician and senior lecturer** [16]

The debate surrounding abortion is complex. It has medical, ethical, theological, social and personal ramifications. The 1967 Abortion Act was a cautious revision of the Infant Life Act of 1929, requiring two practitioners to express their opinion in 'good faith' that to continue the pregnancy would involve either: risk of life to the pregnant mother, risk of injury to her physical and mental health, risk of injury to her existing children's physical and mental health or risk of substantial physical or mental abnormalities to the child. Critics say that the Abortion Law Reform Association clearly didn't predict the consequences of this monumental act, but David Steel, who initiated the bill, affirms that his aim was to 'stamp out backstreet abortions'.

The abortion rate is at its highest for seven years, with 13.2 terminations per 1,000 women, and since 1967 it is approximated that a staggering 5 million babies have been aborted in England and Wales alone. The Office for National Statistics has recently revealed that in the three months to June 1998, there were 43,735 abortions on women living in England and Wales, 973 more than in the same period of 1997. This works out at almost 500 abortions per day.

The rate of abortions continues to climb in almost all age groups, particularly with middle-aged women. A 22 per cent increase was noted in those over the age of forty-five years and an 8 per cent increase in the forty- to forty-four-year-old bracket. The only decrease came among the under-sixteens and the twenty- to twenty-four age range. [17]

According to official figures, eleven out of twelve operations were carried out on grounds of 'risk of injury to the physical or mental health of the woman'. Experts have blamed the increase on the 1995 contraceptive pill scare, where fears were reported that some brands could cause blood clots. Others interpret the rise as a consequence of the introduction of 'lunchtime' abortions, ten-minute procedures which were advertised as minor operations that could be carried out quite easily in a working woman's lunch-hour.

pro-life or pro-choice

> either you accept that the foetus or embryo is a human being with the same rights as a living human being, or you do not. either you believe in a woman's right to choose, or you do not
> — ann furedi [18]

The pro- and anti-abortion campaigners continue to polarise. Pro-life groups believe human life has been trivialised and that the developing foetus is more than just a blob of jelly, it is a human life and deserves the right to live. They are also adamant that evidence points to abortion being traumatically bad for the woman and is a violent death for the developing infant. The pro-life movement wasn't helped a few years ago when Rescue UK took to picketing abortion clinics with pictures of aborted foetuses. Public opinion attested that these shock tactics were more reminiscent of America and many expressed the view that anti-abortion campaigners were crazy, fanatical fundamentalists.

Pro-choice campaigners put the emphasis upon the woman's right to choose and a necessary part of having biological and sexual equality is to have control over your own life and body. Simone De Beauvoir, who took a degree in philosophy at the Sorbonne in 1929, placing second to Jean-Paul Sartre, writes in *The Second Sex*, 'The practical considerations advanced against abortion are without weight; as for the moral considerations, they amount in the end to the old Catholic argument: the unborn child has a soul, which is denied access to paradise if its life is interrupted without baptism. Why should God be forbidden to receive the embryonic soul in heaven?'[19] She continues by pronouncing, 'legal abortion would permit a woman to undertake her maternities in freedom'. [19]

exit

In recent years public opinion has moved towards the acceptance of euthanasia. Supporters argue that every human being should have the right to die in dignity and choose to escape the horrors of a painful and degrading finale. Scientists, doctors and media personalities have supported the legalisation of 'mercy killing'. Those against euthanasia believe that only God has the right to give and take life, and that with compassionate and caring medical attention, there can be a dignity in suffering.

The Voluntary Euthanasia Society wants people 'with a severe illness from which no relief is known' to be allowed to be lawfully killed if they wish. A House of Lords Select Committee will soon recommend if doctors licensed to care should also be licensed to kill.

Legalised euthanasia could become a lazy option and in countries where euthanasia is practised, the hospice facilities are noticeably poor. It is one thing to allow someone, who is incurably on the brink between life and death, to die in dignity, it is another to participate in such a way as to cause or hasten death. Many people are writing down in advance their wishes on what should happen at the end of their lives, and they want it to be legally binding. However, legalised directives will open the door to prosecution if the exact wording is not carried out, and many feel that this route is counter-productive.

The British Medical Association agrees that Living Wills need not be backed by law and recently voted against euthanasia by three to one. The pro-euthanasia lobby see legalised Living Wills as a vital next step to acceptance of euthanasia.

a human being is?

> thomas aquinas set some very clear guidelines on when ensoulment occurs: at 40 days for a male and at 80 days for a female – **rosemary stasek, 'sense of the faithful'**[20]

Everything is up for debate. There is no such thing as an accepted universal truth any more. The discussion surrounding what actually defines a human being is likely to become even more topical and will take centre-stage in most medical and ethical disputes. The public arena has never had to face such giant issues before, and each individual's opinion of what makes a human being human will be the measure for many ethical dilemmas.

The issue becomes even more bizarre when we realise that human-cow clones, or human-monkey clones are on the horizon. By containing human genes, will this animal be considered human and therefore be entitled to human rights? Would it have a soul?

Post-modern novelists and philosophers are turning up the volume, as they broadcast to the world their views on what constitutes a human being. Peter Singer believes that a well-formed animal is superior to a malformed human. His book, *Rethinking Life and Death*, explores his conviction that a person is only a real person when he or she reaches a higher consciousness and self awareness. Francis Crick, the Nobel Prize winning genetic scientist wrote, 'No infant should be declared human until it has passed certain tests regarding its genetic endowment. If it fails these tests, it forfeits the right to live.' [21]

This avant-garde thinking is undermining the very basis of personhood. I fear that in trying to be progressive and enlightened by depersonalising a person, the value of life is being denigrated by a philosophical crusade of ideas, taking the heart and soul out of humanity. This lofty and godless idealism will savagely rape the human species of all identity and destiny, ultimately leaving it destitute.

Bryan Appleyard, in his book *Brave New Worlds: Genetics and Human Experience*, describes how his niece Fiona, born with muscular dystrophy, has challenged his thinking and convictions about human life. In a conversation with Richard Dawkins, evolutionary biologist and author of *The Selfish Gene*, Dawkins stated, 'MD is too terrible to contemplate, it would have been better if Fiona had never been born. We now know enough to stop her happening, and that is what we should do.' Appleyard remarks,

If, before there is a self, there is no person, then it would not have been Fiona that would have been lost in an abortion. But, on the other hand, what would it have been? It could not have been nothing. It must somehow have been part of the human concern. If we consumerise human life, there will be no more Fionas not just because they will be aborted but also because the culture will have lost the spiritual resources to nurture such a human, such a very human being. [22]

> the lord said 'before i formed you in the womb i
> knew you, before you were born i set you apart
> – jeremiah 1:5, the bible, niv version [23]

This avant-garde thinking is undermining the very basis of personhood.

new life

It is interesting that whilst debate continues and becomes more intense with the permitting of experiments on human embryos, and in the future, embryo cloning, there is talk of a new generation of doctors rebelling against the practice of abortion. New 'imaging' techniques show students that the unborn child looks like an unborn child, and not a splodge of tissue. Students are also shocked to discover the cynical ease with which most abortions are granted, most on doubtful 'social grounds'.

Anti-abortion campaigners are finding new life in their convictions amidst growing public unease regarding genetic engineering. The technique of 'selective abortion', the potential of 'designer babies', and the memory of the 1996 destruction of frozen human embryos which had passed their 'use by date' have all added weight to the pro-life perspective.

The world in which we live is changing at a rapid pace with various infertility treatments, surrogacy, egg sharing and innumerable other advances. Dr Patrick Dixon remarks, 'The generation being born now may well be the last to have a "fixed" genetic code, inherited universally in a conventional way. There may well be few alive in thirty years' time who have not had the genetic code of at least some of their cells reprogrammed.' [24]

gene police

> the lesson from history is that whatever can be done, will be done, sometime, somewhere by someone. regulation makes abuse less likely
> – www.globalchange.com [25]

Dr Dixon recommends the introduction of a Gene Charter, 'measures backed by law, designed to protect human safety, to safeguard the environment and to provide ethical standards'. [26] The Charter covers the testing of all new foods by law and requires food labelling to include 'containing products of gene technology'. It also requests viral contamination controls due to the possibility of a viral spread outside the laboratory as a result of genetic research, and a ban on biological warfare research.

The Charter calls, too, for a ban on attempts to alter human cells where the effects could be passed on to future generations and for limits on genetic screening. It aims particularly to make pre-birth genetic screening, where analysis is carried out in order to facilitate the selective destruction of those without desired genetic characteristics, a criminal offence. The Charter covers human cloning and gene therapy, and it demands restrictions on the amount of human genetic code given to an animal, and care for animal welfare so new breeds are healthy. The Charter also suggests that the public should have access to and ownership of information.

Finally the Charter asks for all gene activity to be ethically reviewed by committees incorporating wide public representation, scientific and religious groups.

the big freeze [27]

Some people are now taking extraordinary risks to discover the secret of eternal life. We are beginning to hear of people investing thousands of pounds to have their bodies frozen in the expectation that a way to resurrect them will eventually be found. Cryonics promotes body freezing and according to Christopher Evans, in his article about a British family paying £280,000 to have their bodies (and cats) frozen after they die, the 'British headquarters of Alcor, on the outskirts of Eastbourne, instructs their members to wear bracelets or medallions so that whoever finds them can call a free number in the US'. Evans comments that a devotee of cryonics is 'paying for life after death with a life insurance policy'. [28]

It is amazing the lengths people go to in order to appease their anxiety about eternity. There is an audacious optimism that science will one day conquer and control creation and destiny.

the ethical maze

There are many more issues relating to medical ethics than those delivered here in this word-bite look at trends. The intention of this chapter was never to be an exhaustive study, but rather an informative and chillingly provocative insight into some of the ethical dilemmas which surround us.

Technology will strike unexpectedly. The worst we can do is

ignore the signs of the times, in the vague hope that everything will sort itself out in the end. The best that we can do is adopt an attitude of interest, become informed and measure 'progress' not only with our intellect but with our conscience and with our spirit.

A commentary by Piers Paul Read asks, 'Is this apparent triumph for science also a triumph for humanity? Or is it a step towards the ultimate horror where man usurps the roles of both God and nature and becomes the arbiter of his own creation. It is vital to act before our consciences are numbed.' [29]

> **The best that we can do is adopt an attitude of interest, become informed and measure 'progress' not only with our intellect but with our conscience and with our spirit.**

◎ The observatory look-out

going green

> the world is becoming dirty and ugly, and it's time
> to do something about it. the air is being turned
> into smog. the rivers are polluted. toxic chemicals fill
> the soil. the oceans have become garbage dumps,
> and trash is piling up on the edges of our cities
> **– tony campolo** [1]

There has been, and will continue to be, growing concern about the state of the planet. Talk of the destruction of eco-systems, pollution, global warming, acid rain and resource depletion has filtered through to the conscience of the people. Our planet, once considered strong and durable, has revealed to its inhabitants areas of such weakness, vulnerability and contamination, that alarm bells are ringing.

The key is to be *environmentally aware* and for this awareness to provoke action. Understanding all the statistics and ecological arguments may be slightly advanced for the majority of people, but there is now no excuse for appearing ignorant. Laurence Osborn wrote, 'Ecology is an academic discipline. Environmentalism is a popular response to the perceived threat to the natural environment. Relatively few, active in the environmentalist movement are trained ecologists.' [2]

'Keep Britain Tidy' is more than just a snappy slogan. It was first introduced to keep the country nice and neat, but now pollution has become an issue of life and death. Toxic chemicals, industrial and agricultural waste, insecticides, the commercial packaging of products and groceries, are all enemies of the planet. In addition to these daily threats, we also experience large-scale environmental disasters in the form of nuclear leaks, chemical escapes and oil spills.

We have seen animal and plant species die out due to the loss of, or changes to, their natural habitat. Human greed has chased certain animals into obscurity. Ecosystems have been altered with over a third of the world's tropical rainforests destroyed, and the insatiable demand for energy and raw materials is depleting the earth's resources at an exceptional rate.

... alarm bells are ringing.

eco-warriors

These vast environmental problems can cause us to feel so powerless that we are tempted to opt out. However, an increasing number of people are *opting in*. These eco-warriors are conserving energy, recycling waste, buying environmentally sound products, campaigning for a variety of 'green' issues and genuinely caring about animal life, plant life and the planet's life.

Unlike many indigenous ethical systems, traditional western approaches to the environment have been human-centred. However, that is changing. As holistic becomes mainstream as opposed to alternative, many are actively eco-conscious as a direct result of their own spirituality and beliefs.

The *New Internationalist* magazine explains,

Some are accepting that humans do not always have moral

precedence over other life-forms. The Gaia Hypothesis of James Lovelock suggests that our planet is itself a huge, ruthlessly self-regulating biological organism. It is not committed to the preservation of human life at all. So it may be very much in our interest to convince our planetary host that we are worth keeping on as environmentally conscientious house-guests. [3]

Others embrace the concept of an *earth mother* and worship Gaia, the earth goddess named after 'Terra', the ancient Greek and Roman mythological earth goddess. They express a reverence for the sacred earth and perceive it to be a conscious entity whose processes should be respected and worked with harmoniously. Followers of this religion insist they can merge with nature through meditation and ritual.

Many, however, believe that the world is not a cosmic accident but the product of the activities of a divine creator. Creation-care is linked to a belief in the Christian God who created this world and the universe, along with everything that inhabits the land and the oceans. Campolo explains in his book, *How to Rescue the Earth Without Worshipping Nature*, 'Creation is a trust from God ... God will want to know if we watered it, nurtured it and encouraged its fruitfulness, or if we abused it, forsook it, and ignored its needs.' [4]

We can see that *environmental ethics* are in the process of evolution with various strands emerging. Some are human-centred, some animal-centred, some life-centred and some God-centred. Whatever drives the individual to creation-care will always be varied, but the vitally important element that emerges is that we all must do something, before this planet spins off into destructive oblivion.

These vast environmental problems can cause us to feel so powerless that we are tempted to opt out. However, an increasing number of people are opting in.

nature's bounty

> taxol, a drug derived from bark found in the rain forest, has been tested as a possible preventive for several types of cancer – **tim mcgirk, *time* magazine** 5

In 1998 *Time* magazine announced, 'A primitive tribe in the Andaman Islands off India's eastern coast may have found a cure for malaria, but scientists won't be able to test this potentially life-saving drug anytime soon. The Indian microbiologist who discovered the tribe's "secret" is refusing to publish the formula – to protect the tribe, he says, and to foil his superiors' attempts to profit from it.' 5

There is an increasing quest to track down medically and scientifically useful and 'patentable' substances. Critics call this hunt, 'gene piracy'. Tissue samples from isolated tribes and ethnic communities are also sought after, owing to their unique resistance to certain diseases.

Apparently, around a quarter of all prescription drugs sold in the United States are believed to be based on chemicals derived from only forty plant species, equivalent to 1 per cent of the world's flowering plants. This means that an incredibly large number of plants have not yet been tested for their curable properties, a task made easier due to the advancement of computer and biological technology.

'Bio-sleuths are everywhere,' explains Tim McGirk. 'Everyone, naturally, stands to gain from new treatments that will help people live longer, healthier lives. But the perplexing question is: Who should reap the profits? Everyone wants a piece of the genetic motherlode, and a complex global battle is shaping up over its ownership.' 5

An energy powder, developed by Indian scientists from tribal secrets of the Kani people, has provided them with money for education and medical centres. The researchers agreed to abide by the 1992 United Nations Convention of Biological Diversity and pay the tribe a portion of royalties they receive from commercial drug companies. This novel agreement will hopefully set an ethical precedent, but safeguards are needing to be designed and enforced, so that this type of agreement with the Kani people is not a one-off.

The ethical debate centres around the question of ownership. Who does own nature? A government, a company, a scientist? And will these *discoveries* be heralded as inventions? This debate will continue for a long time because it appears that the intricate and bountiful workings of nature are only just being detected.

the chemical generation

> **sex sells. it may be a cliché, but given the astonishing impact of viagra, few can disagree – *new scientist*** [6]

Technology is tantalising the sexual taste buds.

The arrival of Xcite! is one example of this. If you believe the advertising, these tissues will make you irresistible. They are impregnated with a cocktail of either male or female pheromones, the chemical scent secreted by our bodies to attract a mate, and already nightclubs are installing vending machines for 'wipe-on attraction'. The producers of Xcite! say each wipe carries a warning that it must be used responsibly, but are the makers behaving responsibly by manufacturing the tissues, or is this a money-making scam that is taking the concept of *body chemistry* just a little too far? [7]

Viagra is another example. The diamond-shaped blue wonder

drug, launched in mid-April 1998 in the United States, has exploded onto the international scene, becoming an instant hit and breaking sales' records previously held by the antidepressant, Prozac. In fourteen weeks, two million Viagra prescriptions had been written in the US alone and it quickly established itself as a new recreational drug in club-culture worldwide.

During a trial of the drug then known as UK92-480, a treatment for angina, Pfizer researchers found that many men enrolled on the trial reported improvements in their sex life. Claiming to cure impotence but also to give healthy non-potent older men the sexual performance of a twenty-year-old, Viagra has created a stampede to physicians by a generation of men looking for Viagra-enhanced sex. Dr Derek Machin's prediction that the drug, which is the first oral treatment for impotence, 'could spread like wildfire through the female population' is fast becoming true, and Pfizer has set up an ongoing study of Viagra in European women to find out the benefit.

The social consequences of this drug are alarming enough but the unproven health hazards that accompany it are even more worrying. Few seem concerned about the side effects but figures released in January 1999 have reported sixty-nine deaths in the US alone.

January 1999 was a turning point for Viagra and Britain. The Health Secretary ruled that only men with a narrow range of serious medical problems can get the pills on the NHS. A two-month consultation period was legally necessary before this decision could become permanent. It is estimated that the drug could cost the NHS £100 million a year unless it is restricted. However, the makers of Viagra and many in the medical profession are accusing the government of discriminating against 85 per cent of impotence patients who will not qualify for Viagra on the NHS.

Opposition has been strong from many quarters over the decision to ration Viagra. The British Medical Association said

GPs had an 'ethical and contractual obligation to prescribe to all patients in clinical need, whatever the cause of their impotence'. [8]

In *Women Will Be Wanting Orgasms Next*, Joan Smith writes,

> Orgasms have been established as an inalienable human right, to be prescribed by rebel GPs at tax-payers' expense. It is hard to imagine anyone making a comparable fuss if someone invented a female orgasm pill and the NHS declined to make it freely available to every adult woman in this country who would like to improve her sex life. When the idea of such a drug was mooted a couple of years ago, there was a brief flurry of interest in the media, followed by total silence. [9]

Suzanne Moore goes one step further and comments, 'Society suffers enough from male fantasies paraded as reality. Women who are on the receiving end of all this masculine excitement about Viagra should prepare themselves for the big anti-climax.' [10]

There are those, however, who firmly believe that Viagra should not be available on the NHS at all. Dr Robert Lefevre, a practising GP, comments, 'I am convinced … that the only option will be for the government to say no Viagra can be made available through the NHS. Any half measures will only lead us on to a slippery slope. It will be impossible to stem the demand for Viagra.' [11]

---

it's really a recreational drug that takes all the uncertainty out of the moment. once again, i'm a babe magnet — **hugh hefner, aged 72, *playboy* boss** [12]

this drug is being marketed directly to the ageing 'baby boomer' whose significant other is threatening to get a younger man unless he shapes up — **erica jong** [13]

The Internet is buzzing with demand for Viagra, and the rush for this performance-enhancing drug is rapidly spreading to other nations, creating a lucrative black market. Viagra will become widely used and abused by healthy men and women who have the ability to afford the pills. The impotent will too easily rely on drugs like Viagra rather than put other elements of their life and marriage under the spotlight.

Similar drugs are likely to be introduced onto the market, promising chemical aid for sexual dysfunction. Harin Padma-Nathan of the University of Southern California Medical School explains, 'Viagra has had a revolutionary effect. You're seeing the infancy of a whole new subspecialty of medicine.' [6]

Technology without morality is dangerous, and in a world where sexual performance is receiving high profile, love-making may as well be entered as an olympic sport.

> **Technology without morality is dangerous, and in a world where sexual performance is receiving high profile, love-making may as well be entered as an olympic sport.**

designer medicine

> we live in an age of the lifestyle pill. these days, no man can be too hard, no woman too thin
> – **maureen freely** [14]

A new generation of smart drugs will change society over the next thirty years. They will aim to satisfy the human need for an easy option. Memory-enhancing drugs, stimulatory drugs, fat-busting drugs and drugs to slow down the ageing process will all be introduced.

The popularity of Viagra has alerted drug companies to the need in people for self-improvement. Books, seminars, diets, careful eating and physical exercise appear far too strenuous and demand far too much commitment. In this instant age, people want instant help, and many seem content to put their trust in pills. Writer Erica Jong comments, 'Americans believe in pills much more than they believe in God.' [13]

generation ecstasy

> by the time they're 24, almost half of the british population have taken illegal drugs. recent surveys indicate 2.5 million in england and wales alone have taken speed. 1.3 million have taken acid. 730,000 have taken e. the same number have taken cocaine. 6.3 million have smoked grass – *the face* [15]

Britain has been named the teenage drug abuse centre of Europe. More cannabis and amphetamines are taken here than anywhere else in the EU. Figures have revealed that nearly half of Britain's sixteen- to nineteen-year-olds have taken drugs at some point and more men than women use illegal substances. [16]

Dance drugs or 'hallucinants' are said to have particular appeal to young people and glue sniffing is another endemic problem. Nicholas Saunders in *Ecstasy and the Dance Culture* writes, 'People aren't going to worry about whether or not it's legal to take drugs. They're going to take them if they want to.' [14] Pressure group Parents Against Drug Abuse called the recent findings deeply depressing and commented, 'We are losing the war against drugs.' [16]

Since 1988 there have been around seventy reported deaths in the UK associated with the use of ecstasy in the rave and club scene.

Johnny Davis writes, 'Ecstasy is unique amongst recreational drugs, not least for the feelings of empathy it produces and the social nature of the *ecstasy experience*. Yet the vast majority of writings on ecstasy focus on its toxicity. The most severe reactions include extremely high-temperature fever, convulsions, blood clotting and severe kidney failure – most of which will prove fatal.' [15]

Dr Patrick Dixon in his book, *The Truth About Drugs*, summarises, 'Drug and alcohol abuse is widespread and has a colossal impact in schools, at college and at work. All three places will need to consider urgent introduction of new policies to identify, help and support those with an addiction, and to discourage new users and non-addictive use.' [17]

> the nineties have been a tale of two drugs: one a state-sanctioned happy pill and the other an illegal and evil menace. prozac and ecstasy have a common friend in seratonin, the natural chemical in the brain-stem responsible for mood control, temperature regulation, sensory perception and the onset of sleep – *the face* [18]

food for thought

There is increasing concern over genetically modified (GM) foods. Most of the concern involves the fact that genes are transplanted from animals and even humans, into fruit and vegetables. Fish genes, for example, have been transferred from the Arctic flounder to tomatoes and strawberries to make them frost resistant.

The main GM crops now being grown are soya, maize, cotton and rape. These crops have been made resistant to chemical weed and pest killers, and are therefore able to be sprayed without affecting increasing yields. There is also an environmental risk involved with these crops. There are fears that the GM crops will cross-breed with wild plants to create new plant species which are resistant to conventional chemicals and may eventually ruin large areas of the countryside.

The current food labelling laws mean that shoppers have no guaranteed method of identifying GM products, and they are dependent upon the individual labelling policies of supermarkets. Julie Sheppard from the Consumers' Association remarks, 'The labelling system is a complete shambles. It is so full of loopholes that as much as ninety per cent of GM foods do not have to be labelled.' [19]

A food campaigner for Friends of the Earth, Adrian Bebb, said, 'Time and again consumers have made it clear that they do not want to eat genetically modified food. But little is being done to stop these Frankenstein foods appearing on our plates. It's about time the Government listened to the public rather than the distorted propaganda of the biotech companies.' [19]

Experts around the world are divided on the risks posed by GM foods. There is an obvious concern that in the quest for designer food – where scientists identify genes which control a desired trait, copy them and implant copies into different organisms – human health is threatened.

As the debate continues, and indeed it will long into the new century, there is an urgent need for honesty and clarity. There is also an urgent need for this matter to be discussed by people who do not represent commercial enterprises that stand to gain from the benefits of GM foods. The issue is too important to be determined by commercial pressures. [20]

bodytalk [21]

> your chances in life can be determined by whether
> your body conforms to your society's ideals of
> beauty. it's not just a case of 'you are your body'
> but 'you are what your body looks like'
> **– vanessa baird** [22]

There seems to be an obsession with all things 'bodily' and 'naked'. An evening of television can provide you with programmes on naturists, prostitution and sexual desire all within a limited time slot on a handful of channels only. This is only one element of the world-wide fascination with the human body. Another has been with the shape and size of it, particularly the contours of the female of the species.

The most recent body fashion has been the 'waif' look and major fashion show catwalks have promoted this incredibly thin, physically vulnerable look by configuring their models to this specification. Advertising and Hollywood have contributed to the phenomenon of the 'almost wretched' look, acclaiming it to be a most desired image. Signals are sent quickly to the watching world – to be thin is beautiful and to be fat is undesirable.

The actress Kate Winslet has come to the fore, championing the cause for women who do not fit size 8 or 10. 'I'm not a twig and I refuse to be one. This is me, like it or lump it,' she declares. How brave in a profession where the unspoken law for female stars has been that the more you weigh, the less you'll be paid. Kate's honesty has begun to change opinion and in 1998 she was awarded 'Body of the Year'. Other Hollywood stars have given their support, not prepared any longer to risk health and happiness by conforming to skinny stereotypes. Mia Tyler, half-sister to Liv Tyler, speaks for thousands when she says, 'Beauty comes in all shapes and sizes.'

There is also the possible introduction of Xenical, a wonder drug dieters have dreamed of – a tiny fat-busting pill that gobbles up calories as fast as you can eat them. Obesity is a serious problem in Britain, with almost one in five women and one in seven men risking early death because they are grossly overweight. Demand for Xenical could be far higher than for Viagra. Some are excited by its potential, others are horrified by the consequences. Instead of treating our bodies like temples, critics say we are treating them like laboratories.

> Xenical panders to our modern love of indulgence – the easy fix and instant gratification, without having to pay a price – **fiona whitlock** [23]

Doctors fear that Xenical, which stops the body absorbing around a third of the fat eaten, may be abused by those wanting to lose a few pounds for a holiday or special occasion. 'It may well be that this drug is not only effective if you are too fat, but also if you are a normal weight and want to be slimmer,' says Dr Chisholm of the British Medical Association GPs' Committee. [23]

So what is this fascination with the outside shell that goes beyond the appreciation for the treasure within? Why have we allowed the fashion industry to leave dejected, low self-esteemed victims in its wake? Why does body-consciousness rule supreme even in a world that maintains it's our eternal souls that really count?

Instead of treating our bodies like temples, critics say we are treating them like laboratories.

transformation

> rejuvenate your sex life, discover a whole new world
> of alternative health, double your energy, beat
> stress, unlock your true happiness, fulfil your
> potential, re-awaken your inner self
> – *you* magazine [24]

There will be a continuing emphasis upon self-transformation. From beauty tips to healthy eating, and from hints on how to be happy to overcoming stress, people are aspiring to transcend their present state of self.

Numerous books, videos, recipes, television programmes are all geared towards the search for a better state of mind, body and soul. Self-therapy has almost become the saviour to the masses, as people seek relief from the ailments of third millennium malaise. The success of *The Little Book of Calm* bears witness to this. [25] Written by Paul Wilson to combat sleepless nights and high blood pressure, brought on by the demands of his job, he gives insight into ways of combating stress and bringing calm and serenity into your world. Wilson comments that his doctor recommended medication, but his solution was *meditation.*

People today are far more acquainted with stress and rage than peace and goodwill. Road rage, work rage, supermarket rage, 'on-line' rage (waiting too long for too much useless information), are all symptoms of a culture in crisis. Unpredictable and sometimes fatal, this inability to exercise self-control has created a victim culture. Matathia and Saltzman in their book, *Next,* are predicting that companies will 'monitor and attempt to reduce the stress levels of employees. We'll see everything from on-site aroma-therapy centres and healthy cooking classes to all-expenses paid, company-planned vacations.' [26]

Look out for stress-fighting screensavers which will soon have a measuring device to help reduce tension when there's a work overload!

> **Self-therapy has almost become the saviour to the masses, as people seek relief from the ailments of third millennium malaise.**

size matters

> every day there are thousands of ads that tell young girls they are the wrong shape, the wrong size, the wrong colour, the wrong smell ... they are never told they're remarkable − whether it's in the home or in school − and the curriculum never looks at history from a woman's point of view
> − anita roddick, body shop founder

Western society has been obsessed with the 'perfect figure', more so for women than men. The ascent of the supermodel is evidence enough. These perfect figures have graced many a fashion show and television advert until the message has hit home about what actually constitutes *beauty*. Striving to be the 'perfect 10' or, for the male of the species, the 'handsome hunk' has resulted in low self-worth for those of differing proportions and an increase in eating disorders. Government figures available for 1999 show that one in four fifteen- to sixteen-year-olds are on a diet. New propaganda is finding fast appeal. In particular, the 'Thinking Yourself Slim' methodology whereby neuro-linguistic programming, which is a method of personal analysis, can allegedly shed pounds!

Cosmetic surgery is another growth area, with an increasing number of people changing or enhancing body parts in an effort to simply conform to society's ideal of shape and size. There's a lot of money to be made from notions of what bodies should be like, and a healthy profit is considered more important than an individual's inner peace.

However, size and beauty are being *redefined* as people challenge existing stereotypes. There is even talk that the days of the supermodel are over, with people noticeably gravitating towards *the real look* which represents the majority of the populace. Larger bodies are becoming more acceptable and recognised companies are catering for the fuller figure by incorporating larger sizes within their fashion conscious clothing. Images of larger people, non-white people, disabled people, are being used within advertising campaigns and magazines, positively affirming that the world is made up of varying colours, abilities, looks and sizes and that no one representation is more superior than another.

This will hopefully have a knock-on effect to the countless men and women who have been deeply dissatisfied with themselves due to endless self-comparison with society's ideal image. People need to be released to be themselves rather than persuaded to be someone else.

> **People need to be released to be themselves rather than persuaded to be someone else.**

fashion

> fashion is an imposition, a rein on freedom
> — **golda meir**
>
> fashion is a form of ugliness so intolerable that we have to alter it every six months — **oscar wilde**
>
> fashion is what one wears oneself, what is unfashionable is what other people wear
> — **oscar wilde**

> fashion is dress in which the key feature is rapid
> and continually changing style
> – *new internationalist*

From 'Designer Minimalism' to 'Versace' and from 'Heritage Clothing' to 'Street Sport', one thing is constant: fashion changes. 'To dress fashionably', observes the *New Internationalist* magazine, 'is both to stand out and to merge into the crowd, to lay claim to the exclusive and to follow the herd.' [27]

Designers, analysts and textile specialists put immeasurable time into styling the population, convincing people to adopt the crazy and the sublime, the sophisticated and the functional, in order to make their ideas become trendsetting and, above all, money-making.

There is an uneasy tension between the liberation achieved from self-acceptance and the temptation of transformation. Programmes like the entertaining *Style Challenge* and 'instant makeovers', which emphasise the dreariness of 'the before' and the radiance of 'the after', only serve to feed the frustration people feel with themselves. It's good to care about one's body and hold it to account regarding health and beauty, but let's not be exploited.

Until we become less gullible and more content to choose individuality above conformity, fashion moguls will continue to have the upper hand. Are we going to succumb to the trend for martial arts gear as worn by the Hollywood's hip-list, or to ponyskin clogs and ponchos, or to 'Gucci day-glo bags' or vintage retro excess? Will, as Matathia and Saltzman suggest, future fabrics 'include stress-relieving' qualities and 'aromatherapeutic scents'? Will white become the new black in the year 2000, symbolising purity and simplicity for the new century?

Enjoy fashion, explore fashion, but don't become a slave to it!

Until we become less gullible and more content to choose individuality above conformity, fashion moguls will continue to have the upper hand.

it's good to talk

> your average style hound now worships the mobile, it's the most fashion obliging piece of technology
> – *frank* magazine

Look out for mobile phones becoming the very latest in fashion wear. More than 2.5 million mobile phones were sold in the three months leading up to Christmas 1998, making the number of British users now thirteen million, one in four of the population. [28]

Analysts predict that, in a decade, 90 per cent of all communications will be on the mobile phone. David Chow of *Mobile Choice* magazine comments, 'Ownership is now spread evenly between the genders, with the age of ownership dropping rapidly. The majority are purchased by 20 to 35 year olds, but the children's market will be the next growth area.' [28]

Different colours to suit every outfit, different rings to suit every mood and, in spite of the warnings of brain tumours, the mobile phone is on the up.

paradise on earth [29]

'*Shopping* does something pleasant and satisfying which churches used to do. It brings us together with huge numbers of our fellow humans. It creates a sense of community', commented James Bartholomew in a daily newspaper. [30]

Each week we hear news of another modern-day phenomenon endeavouring to become the new religion. Now it's shopping. This will come as no big surprise because many have already hailed consumerism to be one of the gods of the new age, a way of living that is extremely enticing, promising satisfaction for the soul.

This commentator, however, went one step further as he considered The Trafford Centre, the latest cathedral of shopping opened in Manchester. 'The shopping religion offers paradise on earth – any object you desire from thousands. The shoppers are like members of the congregation.'

Shopping malls all over Britain attract more visitors, or devotees, than churches. A tragic but true fact. Tragic because the eternal significance of the latest gadget or garment bears absolutely no comparison with the eternal significance of a true spiritual union. And yet on the surface this shopping religion is charismatically inviting to all ages and its advertising is impressively evangelistic.

How far will people go to find paradise on earth? Well, as far as the Internet can take them! The potential of this electronic shop window is immense and has huge ramifications for existing methods of buying and selling. Soon, everything will become available on-line from food to holidays, books to cyberbanking, and lifestyle pills to sperm donors. Custom music CDs can be created and downloaded leaving record shops to wonder upon their future. Live events can be broadcast 'on-line' threatening concert attendances, and with more homes having ISDN connections, electronic trading will be accomplished from the comfort of your own lounge, watching your own TV.

How far will people go to find paradise on earth? Well, as far as the Internet can take them!

love@aol

You've Got Mail, starring Meg Ryan and Tom Hanks, tells an increasingly familiar story of on-line dating and cyberspace love. The manager of AOL comments, 'More people will want to date on-line once they see this movie.' [31]

Matchmaking sites are gaining an increasing number of hits and one such site, Match.com, is reporting 20,000 new singles every week. 'There is a website to suit every taste however eclectic or bizarre', writes Tom Rhodes, 'and the ability of companies to deliver results has become an extraordinary by-product of the high-tech revolution. The premise is that on-line courtship circumvents conventions and pretensions.' [31]

E-mail relationships can be far more intimate than normal dating, with women being the most likely to find a potential lover on-line. An American study found that 33 per cent of all on-line relationships led to a date.

This hi-tech cyberworld is overflowing with opportunity and is successfully eradicating the need to go outside your front door; even romance can blossom without the old-fashioned need to get out and meet people. The screen has become the modern-day dance floor where modems move to the rhythm of 56k bps and where the language of love takes the shape of an e-mail rather than an intimate gaze. As the use of the Internet doubles every year or so, the number of e-mail relationships will explode.

addicted to love

Relationships, as we all know, take time to develop and on-line love may encourage people to get even more hooked on the Internet. The Center for Online Addiction (COLA), is believed to be the first 'virtual clinic' to treat a phenomenon known as

'Internet Addiction Disorder'. The symptoms include a sense of euphoria when switching on your terminal, lying about the amount of time spent on the Internet, irritability and anxiety when not engaged in computer activities, a constant refusal to quit and a failure to maintain personal hygiene. Apparently Britain has half a million weboholics.

Where will all this lead us? Will we eventually discover a whole generation of technophiles unable to develop face-to-face relationships, inept at group interchange and in desperate need of advice regarding interpersonal relating skills? Will we enter an age of cyberdating that sees an escalation in 'multiple dating', virtual 'agony aunts' and the normalisation of cybersex?

In this techno-age, let us not lose sight of the value of relationships and community, not virtual but REAL.

game on

Look out for even greater advances in the realm of home entertainment, interactive CDs, DVDs and computer games for children and adults.

Sega's new video game console 'Dreamcast' is currently the world's most powerful, based around a 128-bit Hitachi console. Although intended primarily for gaming, the Dreamcast uses a custom version of Microsoft Windows CE and includes a built-in modem. This means the Dreamcast could well be used for such applications as web browsing and e-mail.

Video games are increasingly pushing back the boundaries of creativity with some amazing high-tech platform games. Concern is being expressed, however, at the content of such games, with a high proportion depicting violence, destruction and death. 'Wargasm', for example, has been described as 'an action-packed arcade style wargame that will appeal to destructive folk the world over,' and the advertising for *Duke Nukem: Time to Kill,* entices us to 'embark upon an unadulterated adventure in sex, violence and chewin' gum ... and enjoy the wonders of this delightfully sordid romp'. [32]

The signs of excess are already evident.

public displays of confession [33]

Imagine you have been secretly living a lie for years and no one knows; or perhaps you have a history of deceiving people to obtain their life savings. Well, the time has come to own up and confess.

One would assume that the best place for such sensitive and emotional disclosures is in private. Surely the most suitable location to cope with the shame, the anger, the embarrassment, the possible forgiveness and restitution would be away from prying eyes. But oh no ... modern living has a better idea. If you have something to divulge, then shout it out to as many people as possible.

Television talk shows have become modern-day confessionals where media-priests religiously perform their duties, providing a platform for ordinary people to expose their sins and face the person whom they have sinned against. This is the moment of truth – is there absolution for the sinner? Often there are tears, verbal abuse, violence, strong feelings of betrayal but rarely absolution. The watching crowd love the fights, the raised voices and the visible shame – and the more debasing the confession, the better the spectacle. This is television at its best, or is it?

The host of America's most talked about talk show is Jerry Springer. The programme is watched by millions and is now being copied in Britain, where elements of Springer are creeping into what were once interesting discussion shows, turning them into sensationalistic sideshows. With titles like 'Honey I'm really a guy' or 'My sister slept with my three boyfriends', the viewer becomes a voyeur – left to wrestle with a distinct feeling of awkwardness and a fascination to know how it's all going to end! Once we get the taste for public displays of confession, will we reject it or become addicted? Does this spell danger for Britain and what can we do about it?

The easy answer is that if we feel these talk shows are degrading, then *don't* watch them. If ratings slip and letters are written by offended viewers, then producers should take notice. The Springer Show in America has regularly incurred public wrath, inciting the executives to make claims promising to curb the language and the violence. To date, these appear empty promises, but chances are they care more about ratings than they do about the people who appear on their shows.

Television talk shows have become modern-day confessionals ...

a religious image

Fashion is appropriating religious imagery and designers, according to Margit J. Mayer, 'have long been wise to the seductive cocktail of visual splendour and spiritual rigour associated with the church.' [34]

It is also interesting how much religious language and symbolism is continually being used in mainstream music. An Australian band adopts the name SuperJesus, there is an album called *Spirit Tales*, Ash has a song entitled 'Jesus Says', and The Verve have the brilliant album *Urban Hymns*.

A flyer for a dance club invites the masses to be 'Serious at the Cross', the Cross being a London location, and the excellent song 'God is a D.J.', by Faithless, compares church with dance culture in that both environments are meeting people's needs. The Ministry of Sound who wanted to oust religion from the Millennium Dome remarked, 'Dance tunes are like hymns to young people and clubs are the churches of the millennium.' [35]

The fashion line Ted Baker commands, 'Do not worship false labels', tattoo kits contain Christian Celtic symbolism and an advert for Soccernet reads, 'If you believe that Saturday afternoons are sacred. If you worship a team or a player. If you recite the offside rule as a litany. Then you should make a pilgrimage to Soccernet.'

Why this fascination with Christian language and symbolism? Mayer concludes, 'One reason might be a creeping ennui with lofty New Age philosophers and their somewhat vague pointers to happiness.' [34]

Look out for more 'western spirituality merged with eastern spirituality' inspired fashion.

icons and idols

Everyone has the capacity to adore something or someone and to follow their idol with a passionate commitment.

Brian Harvey, ex East 17 vocalist, was an example of how the pop scene penetrated national culture. His words of support for the designer drug ecstasy added fuel to the already considerable fire of experimentation practised each week. The Spice Girls are another example, hailed as apostles of this age for thousands of pre-pubescent girls. According to their management, 'they connect with them and share the same values'. In other words, 'They tell them what they want, what they really, really want.' [36]

Worship is alive and well on planet earth, with most of today's idols immersed within the music, movies or sports scene. Regular features in magazines, television appearances and Internet information allow their words and lifestyle to have a profound effect upon a generation in the process of shaping their own value system and behavioural code.

Music, for example, is a global language with an incredible power to communicate. What is disturbing is the 'publicity machine' that indiscriminately elevates singers and songwriters to 'god-like' status in the eyes of their followers. In the midst of the more prevalent 'bump 'n' grind' stimuli, where are the voices singing out for dignity and purity? Can anyone offer an alternative to the stream of narcissistic ideology that storms the charts? Does anyone of influence *really* care about the diet fed to developing minds?

New role-models are desperately needed. Culture-shapers who will broadcast a different value system based upon selflessness and a respect for others.

Worship is alive and well on planet earth …

fake society

Faking It: The Sentimentalism of Modern Society, is a series of essays by academics on our 'self-indulgent civilisation'. The book concludes, 'It is a fake society with fake institutions. It has buildings that look like schools but with no real education inside them; churches attended by congregations seeking cosy self-esteem rather than an encounter with Almighty God.' [37]

The book also contains an essay by Anthony O'Hear, a philosophy professor, who criticises Princess Diana, claiming that her funeral was the defining moment of this new sentimentality when 'mob grief was personified and the sacrificial victim was canonised'. [38]

Opinions vary regarding the 'People's Princess'. Walking

around Kensington Gardens soon after the tragedy, I was profoundly touched by the thousands of people, young and old, deeply impacted by Diana's death. The flowers on the streets and surrounding the palaces were not only a magnificent sight but the fragrance was intoxicating. Since the death of Jesus, has any other death had such an overwhelming impact on the world? Why did people feel so much grief? Why did people search within themselves and feel such a void?

Many seemed to touch and re-visit their own personal sadnesses and losses whilst mourning Diana. At the same time, however, many lamented the loss of a vulnerable woman who reached out to the socially excluded, the AIDS victims and the lepers, the children and the homeless. Lord St John of Fawsley remarked, 'Her appeal lay precisely in that she elevated feeling to the highest position.' [38]

Critics have derided the very public show of emotion, the 'touchy-feely' sentimentality that was displayed over Diana. But I applaud it. I respect the street-shrines, created in honour of someone's untimely death or a regional disaster. For too long we have hidden our feelings behind a private mask, and through our silence and inability to be real about our emotions, we have contributed to what some people describe as a 'fake society'.

Ann Leslie comments, 'Perhaps unwittingly – perhaps indeed, undeservedly – she not only personified a cultural change, but drove it forward into the new millennium.' [39] In this post-Diana age, the greatest accolade we can give the People's Princess is to promise to be real.

For too long we have hidden our feelings behind a private mask ...

◎ Promise Land [40]

a light's gone out in the world today,
storm clouds have come our way
and hidden our smiles from view,
and even the sun is weeping

flowers on the streets today
from palace to motorway
the fragrance of emptiness
is everywhere, everywhere

> but if we dare to hope for better days
> we will hear the cry of the powerless
> for peace and faith to come to this promise land
> and if we dare to pray for better days
> we will find our way through the wilderness
> peace and faith will come to this promise land

oh comfort, comfort Your people
hear us when we call
your will be done on earth
as it is in heaven

but if we dare to hope for better days
we will hear the cry of the powerless
for peace and faith to come to this promise land
and if we dare to pray for better days
we will find our way through the wilderness
peace and faith will come to this promise land

caroline bonnett/sue rinaldi

from the album 'promise land' by sue rinaldi on
survivor records

trendthe resource file

the making of trend   resourcefile

1   colin jarman, *the guinness dictionary of more poisonous quotes* (guinness, 1992) p. 37

2   steve sutherland, *from teds to mods to hippies to skins to goths to this* (new musical express, 5 dec 1998)

3   clive aslet, *isn't it time to celebrate maturity rather than worship the cult of youth* (the daily mail, 4 oct 1997)

4   ira matathia & marian salzman, *? next* (harpercollins, 1999) p. xii

5   john drane, *faith in a changing culture* (marshall pickering, 1997) p. 41

6   margit j mayer, *god only knows* (frank magazine, dec 1998)

7   harriet quick, *letter from frank* (frank magazine, dec 1998)

8   margit j mayer, *god only knows* (frank, dec 1998)

9   roger ellis & chris seaton, *new celts* (kingsway, 1998) p. 14

10   ellis/seaton, *new celts* (kingsway, 1998) p. 14

11   ellis/seaton, *new celts* (kingsway, 1998) p. 7

12   richard appignanesi & chris garratt, *postmodernism for beginners* (icon, 1995) p. 136

13   appignanesi/garratt, *postmodernism for beginners* (icon, 1995) p. 126

14   douglas coupland, *generation x* (abacus, 1991)

15   polly wilson (adelaide news, oct 1998)

16   paul waugh, *mixed-up youth of the millennium* (the independent, 14 nov 1998)

17   rupert howe, *new adventures in sci-fi* (the face, dec 1998)

spiritzone <small>resourcefile</small>

1 sue rinaldi, *culture vulture* (new christian herald, 7 jun 1997)

2 william raeper & linda smith, *a beginner's guide to ideas* (lion, 1991) p. 61

3 raeper/smith, *a beginner's guide to ideas* (lion, 1991) p. 63

4 raeper/smith, *a beginner's guide to ideas* (lion, 1991) p. 66

5 richard england, *the spirit of place* (l'arcaedizioni, 1998) p. 12

6 jonathan petre & macer hall, *high on drugs, low on hope* (the sunday telegraph, 27 dec 1998)

7 miranda sawyer, *ideals for living* (the face, jan 1997)

8 richard england, *the spirit of place* (l'arcaedizioni, 1998) p. 40

9 paul gordon, *secular thoughts* (the guardian, 30 dec 1998)

10 sue rinaldi, *culture vulture* (new christian herald, 6 jun 1998)

11 james clark, *taking christianity out of a christening* (the daily mail, 6 may 98)

12 enigma, *m c m x c a.d* (virgin records, 1990)

13 madeleine bunting, *priests who can deliver us from evil* (the guardian, 30 dec 1998)

14 *predictions 1999* (frank magazine, jan 1999)

15 billy graham, *angels* (hodder & stoughton, 1987) p. 30

16 theolyn cortens, *angels in languedoc* (a divine retreat, july 1993)

17 jonathan cainer, *new age stargazers?* (the daily mail, 14 nov 1996)

18 natalie clarke, *the power of the paranormal* (the daily mail, 2 feb 1998)

19 sue rinaldi, *culture vulture* (new christian herald, 6 sept 1997)

20 solara, *11:11 the opening of the doorway* (aristia, jan 1992)

21 jane kelly, *the year 2000* (the daily mail, 29 dec 1998)

22 cam winstanley, *seize the day, interview with robin williams* (total film, jan 1999)

23 jonathan petre, *drag queen preacher to present bbc show* (the sunday telegraph, 27 dec 1998)

24 joshua cooper ramo, *finding god on the web* (time magazine, 16 dec 1996)

25 russell miller, *the true story of a false prophet* (night + day, 30 mar 1997)

26 sue rinaldi, *culture vulture* (new christian herald, 5 sept 1998)

27 ivor key, *gospel of good health* (the daily mail, 5 sept 1998)

28 charles strohmer, *comment* (dec 1998), *what your horoscope doesn't tell you* (word, 1991), *explaining the grace of god* (sovereign world, 1993), *wise as a serpent, harmless as a dove* (word, 1994), *building bridges to the new age world* (cpas, 1996)

29   gerald coates, *millennium melt down?* (pioneer, jan 1997)
30   ann treneman, *the reverend revolutionaries* (the independent, 7 jan 1999)
31   alan travis, *2001 census will put faith in religious beliefs* (the guardian, 4 jan 1999)

healing waters   resourcefile

1   roger ellis, *the new age and you* (kingsway)
2   diana bagnall, *natural progression* (newsweek, 3 nov 1998)
3   eileen fletcher, *medicine or magic?* (new consciousness, 1)
4   samuel pfeifer, *healing at any price?* (word, 1988) pp. 29–30
5   eleanor bailey, *plug into healing power* (you magazine, 6 sept 1997)
6   natalie clarke, *the power of the paranormal* (the daily mail, 2 feb 1998)
7   anna pasternak, *in good hands* (style, jan 1999)
8   dr m duke, *acupuncture* (pyramid house, 72) p. 164
9   david derbyshire, *pine tree drug* (the daily mail, jan 1999)
10   bach flower remedies, *pamphlet* (bach remedies)
11   david bainbridge, david fitzgerald & david adam, *the eye of the eagle* (kingsway music, 1998)
12   raeper/smith, *a beginner's guide to ideas* (lion, 1991) p. 104
13   john drane, *what is the new age saying to the church* (marshall pickering, 1991) p. 59
14   john drane, *what is the new age saying to the church* (marshall pickering, 1991) p. 60
15   dan millman, *everyday enlightenment* (hodder & stoughton, 1998) p. 6
16   lillian too, *little book of feng shui* (element, 1998)

the sexual explosion I   resourcefile

1   sue rinaldi, *culture vulture* (new christian herald, 1 mar 1997)
2   steve doughty, *the child mothers* (the daily mail, 11 dec 1998)

3   dr patrick dixon, *the rising price of love* (hodder & stoughton, 1995) p. 3

4   dr patrick dixon, *the rising price of love* (hodder & stoughton, 1995) p. 3–4

5   simon andreae, *anatomy of desire* (little, brown, 1998) p. 34

6   michael mason, *the making of victorian sexual attitudes* (oup, 1994)

7   dr patrick dixon, *the rising price of love* (hodder & stoughton, 1995) p. 5

8   bruce anderson, *just what can britain learn from the past?* (the daily mail, 26 oct 1996)

9   simon andreae, *anatomy of desire* (little, brown) p. 35

10 simon andreae, *anatomy of desire* (little, brown) p. 128

11 lynda lee-potter, *high street shelves of shame* (the daily mail, 17 nov 1989)

12 william masters & virginia johnson, *human sexual response* (little, brown, 1966)

13 dr patrick dixon, *the rising price of love* (hodder & stoughton, 1995) p. 6

14 joan smith, *different for girls* (chatto & windus, 1997) p. 21

15 jenne liburd, *are you soft on porn?* (sibyl magazine, july/aug 1998)

16 steve chalke/nick page, *sex matters* (hodder & stoughton, 1996) p. 10

17 anouk ride, *another planet* (new internationalist, july 1998)

18 harvey marcus, *sex and the city* (frank, jan 1999)

19 mary kenny, *are we betraying our teenagers?* (the daily mail, 15 oct 1993)

20 joyce hopkirk, *why I deplore this obsession with sex* (the daily mail, 12 oct 1995)

21 helen somerville, *assess critically christian objections to pornography* (report, 1998)

22 miranda sawyer & adam higginbottom, *how much porn can you take* (select, sept 1994)

23 jim harding, *the end of alice* (the daily mail, 27 oct 1997)

24 philip elmer-dewitt, *on a screen near you* (time magazine, 3 july 95)

25 anthony daniels, *the royal academy is degrading us all* (the daily mail, 17 sept 1997)

26 paul johnson, *will decency or decadence triumph in british life?* (the daily mail, 20 sept 1997)

27 christopher tookey, *film that tells perverts all they want to hear* (the daily mail, 22 sept 1997)

28   rhys williams, *too much sex on the tv* (the independent, 7 jan
      1999)
29   anne atkins, *what kind of society* (the daily mail, 24 april 1997)

the sexual explosion **II**   resourcefile

1   sue rinaldi, *culture vulture* (new christian herald, 7 mar 1998)
2   simon andreae, *anatomy of desire* (little, brown, 1998) p. 130
3   william oddie, *under age* (the daily mail, 7 march 1998)
4   angela lambert, *blame society* (the daily mail, 11 dec 1998)
5   steve doughty, *shock rise in schoolgirl babies* (the daily mail, 11 dec
      1998)
6   neil sears, *schoolgirls sex clinic* (the daily mail, 10 dec 1998)
7   uncredited, *under-age sex must never be accepted* (the daily mail, 11
      dec 1998)
8   pearl assurance, *girls say marriage and motherhood is not for them*
      (the daily mail, 21 sept 1998)
9   steve doughty, *office for national statistics* (the daily mail, 11 dec
      1998)
10   jonathan leake, *pink pound powers gay house boom* (the sunday
      times, 10 aug 1997)
11   carla power, *the outing of europe* (newsweek, 23 nov 1998)
12   lewis wolberg, *homosexuality* (encarta 95)
13   debrief, *queenie* (everywoman, july 1996)
14   james clark, *couples sought for adoption* (the daily mail, 8 dec 1998)
15   uncredited, *lesbians order a baby on the net* (the daily mail, 10 july
      1998)
16   leo mckinstry, *how tv has helped destroy the family* (the daily mail,
      29 dec 1998)
17   christopher morgan, *carey friend threatens church split by blessing
      gay marriage* (the times, july 1997)
18   james langton, *thongs of praise* (the sunday telegraph, 3 nov 1996)
19   martin scott, *the bible and homosexuality* (booklet, 1997) p. 18–22
20   elaine storkey, *the search for intimacy* (hodder & stoughton, 1995)
      p. 201
21   aids care, education and training (acet), *securing the future* (review
      1997–1998)

22   dr patrick dixon, *the rising price of love* (hodder & stoughton, 1995) p. 71

23   sue rinaldi, *fast-moving currents in youth culture* (lynx, 1995) p. 107

24   various, *a lost generation* (newsweek, 18 jan 1993)

25   dr patrick dixon, *the genetic revolution* (kingsway, 1993) p. 132

26   paul waugh, *mixed-up youth of the millennium* (the independent, 14 nov 1998)

27   melanie mcfadyean, *just say no* (night & day, 3 jan 1999)

gendertalk   resourcefile

1   sue rinaldi, *culture vulture* (new christian herald, 3 may 1997)

2   leo mckinstry, *the real reason why men are behaving badly* (the daily mail, 26 aug 1998)

3   elaine storkey, *what's right with feminism* (spck, 1985) p. 134

4   harriet beecher stowe, *uncle tom's cabin*

5   uncredited, *the facts* (new internationalist, aug 95)

6   lucy o'brien, *material girl* (sibyl, mar/april 1998)

7   christopher morgan & sarah toyne, *queen resists women priests in her chapels* (the sunday times, 20 dec 1998)

8   natasha walter, *the new feminism* (little, brown, 1998)

9   prudential, *FIT and paying her way* (survey, nov 1998)

10   various, *what women want* (virago, 1996)

11   alan jackson, *girlzone* (the times, 18 jan 1997)

12   various, *righteous babes* (bbc2, dec 1998)

13   bel mooney, *why i deplore so many of today's women* (the daily mail, 10 july 1998)

14   statistics (new internationalist, 1997–98)

15   simon andreae, *anatomy of desire* (little, brown, 1998) p. 94

16   simone de beauvoir, *the second sex* (vintage, 1997) p. 112

17   elaine storkey, *contributions to christian feminism* (christian impact, 1995)

18   phil moore, *take a bishop like me* (1979)

19   mary daly, *beyond god the father* (the women's press, 86) p. 19

20   *the bible*, genesis 1 verse 27

21   martin scott, *the redemptiveness of male imagery* (privately
      published essay, 1997)
22   mother julian of norwich, *revelations of divine love* (hodder &
      stoughton, 1987) p. 129

genderquake   resourcefile

1   simon andreae, *anatomy of desire* (little, brown, 1998)
      pp. 144–145
2   zachary l nataf, *whatever i feel* (new internationalist, april 1998)
3   angela levin, *from joel to joella* (the daily mail, 8 dec 1998)
4   james clark, *taxpayers must foot the bill* (the daily mail, 22 dec
      1998)
5   matt ridley, *the red queen* (viking, 1993)
6   various, *our bodies ourselves* (boston women's health, 71)
7   julie burchill, *i knew i was smart* (the guardian, 4 april 1998)
8   elaine storkey, *the search for intimacy* (hodder & stoughton, 1995)
      pp. 120 –123
9   zarina banu, *ooh, ah, female footy stars* (sibyl, sept/oct 98)
10   ron stodghill II, *god of our fathers* (time, 13 oct 1997)
11   myfanwy franks, *marriage, obedience and feminine submission*
      (privately published essay, 1998)
12   jenny baker, *women and men in ministry* (report for Youth for
      Christ, 1995)
13   joan smith, *different for girls* (chatto & windus, 1997) pp. 79–81
14   shulamith firestone, *the dialectic of sex* (jonathan cape, 1971)
15   victoria owen, *family futures report* (the daily mail, 19 dec 1998)

single minded   resourcefile

1   marcus berkmann, *two's company, one's an outcast* (the daily mail,
      23 jan 1990)
2   elaine storkey, *the search for intimacy* (hodder & stoughton, 1995)

3 elaine storkey, *the search for intimacy* (hodder & stoughton, 1995) p. 207

4 kate jackson, *why did i put up with this man for ten years* (you magazine, 31 mar 1998)

5 ian stuart gregory, *no sex please we're single* (kingsway, 1997)

6 lowri turner, *hip singles* (elle, 1998)

7 deborah holder, *the singles epidemic* (options, may 1997)

8 sarah kennedy & nicola gill, *strong, happy and single* (cosmopolitan, oct 1998)

9 linda harding, *better than or equal to?* (word/pioneer, 1993)

10 sue rinaldi, *culture vulture* (new christian herald, 5 april 1997)

11 sally cline, *women, celibacy and passion* (optima, 1993)

12 eugene peterson, *the message* (navpress, 1994) romans 12 verse 1

13 lina das & jenny nisbet, *no sex please* (the daily mail, 21 mar 1997)

14 yvonne roberts, *the trouble with single women* (pan, 1998)

15 angela lambert, *will you be lonesome tonight?* (the independent, 19 oct 1995)

ethics – a snapshot   resourcefile

1 sue rinaldi, *culture vulture* (new christian herald, 2 aug 1997)

2 celia hall & joy copley, *an abortion in your lunch-hour* (the times, aug 1997)

3 p baelz, *ethics and belief* (sheldon press, 1977)

4 greg valerio, *where revival and justice meet* (compass, autumn 1998)

5 vanessa baird, *how are we to live?* (new internationalist, april 1997)

6 peter singer, *the drowning child and the expanding circle* (new internationalist, april 1997)

7 david ransom, *jeans, the big stitch-up* (new internationalist, june 1998)

8 uncredited, *ethical consumerism* (ethical consumer, july 1995)

9 richard swift, *chocolate saves the world* (new internationalist, aug 1998)

10 dr patrick dixon, *the genetic revolution* (kingsway, 1993) p. 15

11 paul johnson, *my fears for our future* (the daily mail, 2 jan 1999)

12 david derbyshire, *dawn of the frankenstein age* (the daily mail, 9 dec 1998)

13 dr jacqueline laing, *dawn of the frankenstein age* (the daily mail, 9 dec 1998)

14 david derbyshire, *the first human clone* (the daily mail, 17 dec 1998)

15 dr patrick dixon, *the genetic revolution* (kingsway, 1993) p. 182

16 dr tony cole, *why shouldn't we doctors make moral judgements?* (the daily mail, 16 nov 1998)

17 office for national statistics, *figures for 1998*

18 decca aitkenhead, *new lease of life* (the independent, 11 aug 1996)

19 simone de beauvoir, *the second sex* (vintage, 1997) pp. 503–510

20 rosemary stasek, *sense of the faithful* (new internationalist, july 1998)

21 elaine storkey, *culture change* (seminar, sept 1998)

22 bryan appleyard, *brave new worlds: genetics and the human experience* (harpercollins, 1998)

23 *the bible*, jeremiah 1 verse 5

24 dr patrick dixon, *the genetic revolution* (kingsway, 1993) p. 18

25 global change, *www.globalchange.com*

26 dr patrick dixon, *the genetic revolution* (kingsway, 1993) pp. 183–191

27 sue rinaldi, *culture vulture* (new christian herald, 2 jan 1998)

28 christopher evans, *the secret of eternal youth* (the daily mail, 12 dec 1998)

29 piers paul read, *act to halt this evil before it's too late* (the daily mail, 17 dec 1998)

the observatory — lookout   resourcefile

1 tony campolo, *how to rescue the earth without worshipping nature* (word, 1992) pp. 9–10

2 lawrence osborn, *guardians of creation* (apollos, 1993)

3 various, *lofty ideas or just hot air?* (new internationalist, april 1997)

4 tony campolo, *how to rescue the earth without worshipping nature* (word, 1992) p. 194

5 tim mcgirk, *dealing in dna* (time magazine, 30 nov 1998)

6   neil boyce, *sexual healing* (new scientist, dec/jan 1999)

7   sue rinaldi, *culture vulture* (new christian herald, 1 aug 1998)

8   emily wilson, *showdown on viagra* (the daily mail, 23 jan 1999)

9   joan smith, *women will be wanting orgasms next* (the independent, 24 jan 1999)

10   suzanne moore, *when an old banger loses his sex drive* (the mail on sunday, 24 jan 1999)

11   dr robert lefevre, *why viagra should never be available on the nhs* (the daily mail, 22 jan 1999)

12   michael sheldon, *once again i'm a babe magnet* (the daily telegraph, 27 july 1998)

13   erica jong, *it's hard to please everyone* (the guardian, april 1998)

14   maureen freely, *that won't hurt a bit* (article, oct 1998)

15   johnny davis, *bad medicine* (the face, april 1998)

16   uncredited, *britain's teens top the euro-drugs league* (the daily mail, 4 dec 1998)

17   dr patrick dixon, *the truth about drugs* (hodder & stoughton, 1998) p. 37

18   various, *50 revolutions per minute* (the face, jan 1997)

19   david hughes, *genetic food watch* (the daily mail, 6 feb 1999)

20   comment, *an issue of concern* (the daily mail, 6 feb 1999)

21   sue rinaldi, *culture vulture* (new christian herald, 5 dec 1998)

22   vanessa baird, *the world made flesh* (new internationalist, april 1998)

23   fiona whitlock, *the fat-busting pill* (article, oct 1998)

24   various, *the new you* (you magazine, jan 1999)

25   paul wilson, *the little book of calm* (penguin, 1998)

26   ira matathia & marian salzman, *? next* (harpercollins, 1999) p. 48

27   elizabeth wilson, *adorned in dreams* (virago, 1985)

28   libby brooks, *if you don't have one yet, you will soon* (the guardian, 9 jan 1999)

29   sue rinaldi, *culture vulture* (new christian herald, 3 oct 1998)

30   james bartholomew, *has shopping become the new religion?* (the daily mail, 15 sept 1998)

31   tom rhodes, *cyber lovers* (the sunday times, 20 dec 1998)

32   news, *buyers queue up* (what pc, feb 1999)

33   sue rinaldi, *culture vulture* (new christian herald, 4 april 1998)

34   margit j mayer, *god only knows* (frank, dec 1998)

35   teletext, *millennium dome*

36   sue rinaldi, *culture vulture* (new christian herald, 1 feb 1997)

37   various, *faking it : the sentimentalisation of modern society*
     (Penguin, 1998)
38   sonia purnell, *cry-baby britain* (the daily mail, 17 april 1998)
39   ann leslie, *i at last understand those to whom she is a saint* (the daily
     mail, 29 aug 1998)
40   caroline bonnett & sue rinaldi, *promise land* (survivor records,
     april 1998) 01932 232312

other resources from sue rinaldi

promise land (survivor records, 1998) – SURCD005
love eternal (kingsway, 1994) – KMCD730
news and info from: soundhouse
email: soundhouse@clara.net
website: www.soundhouse.clara.net

sue rinaldithe lowdown

Born in Southampton, Sue trained in accountancy before going freelance as a singer-songwriter and communicator.

Travelling internationally as an artist/communicator, she was lead vocalist for the band Heartbeat between 1986 and 1991 and co-wrote the band's two chart singles – 'Tears from Heaven' and 'The Winner' – which led to several TV appearances including *Top of the Pops*, *The Roxy* and *Daytime Live*. Much experience has been accumulated in the realm of recording and performing, and as a session artist.

Sue performed at Wembley Arena as part of the GMTV/NSPCC Christmas Show and in June 1996 was the presenter for Champion of the World, also at Wembley Arena. July 1997 saw her perform with her band for Champion of the World – Part 2 at Wembley Stadium in front of an international crowd of fifty thousand.

An artist and guest on various TV programmes including the *Sunday Programme*, on GMTV, and the Channel 4 documentary *God in the House*, which was screened on Christmas Day 1997, Sue has also given a highly acclaimed presentation of Christian views on contemporary issues on DEF 11's *A–Z of Belief*. As a presenter for many national and international events and a regular contributor to radio, she has also travelled to Brazil to co-present a video highlighting the plight of abandoned children around the world and has also appeared in *Doorways to Danger* – a video for schools on the subject of the occult.

Her second solo album *Promise Land* had a Spring 1998 release date. Ambient and rhythmic, beautiful and moving, *Promise Land* delivers a rich landscape of sound and great songs. This album has received outstanding reviews with live performances around Britain and other nations including an extremely positive tour of Australia in the Autumn of 1998.

Her first solo album *Love Eternal* was released in 1994. From dance to acoustic, this energetic collection of songs expresses a love and devotion for God whilst exploring the social context of the world we live in. The album has received high acclaim from record companies, press reviews and listeners and has been released in the USA under the N.Soul label and has also been repackaged and released in Australia.

For many years Sue has been leading and co-ordinating worship and has written and co-written many songs which are currently being used around the world. Her time is also spent communicating about today's issues and she has contributed to *Fast Moving Currents in Youth Culture*, a book examining youth and current trends. As a regular contributor to *Christian Herald* she comments into their 'CultureWatch' series. She also gives specialist seminars and workshops under the title of 'The Voice Factory' which cover vocal training and performing.